Rover

OTHER BOOKS BY BARRY BLACKSTONE

Though None Go With Me
Rendezvous In Paris
Though One Go With Me
Scotland Journey
The Region Beyond
Enlarge My Coast
From Dan to Beersheba and Beyond
The Uttermost Part
Homestead Homilies

ROVER

A Boy's Best Friend

Barry Blackstone

RESOURCE *Publications* • Eugene, Oregon

ROVER
A Boy's Best Friend

Copyright © 2017 Barry Blackstone. All rights reserved. Except for brief quotations in critical publications or reviews, no part of this book may be reproduced in any manner without prior written permission from the publisher. Write: Permissions, Wipf and Stock Publishers, 199 W. 8th Ave., Suite 3, Eugene, OR 97401.

Resource Publications
An Imprint of Wipf and Stock Publishers
199 W. 8th Ave., Suite 3
Eugene, OR 97401

www.wipfandstock.com

PAPERBACK ISBN: 978-1-5326-3433-8
HARDCOVER ISBN: 978-1-5326-3435-2
EBOOK ISBN: 978-1-5326-3434-5

Manufactured in the U.S.A.

I dedicate this series of remembrances of my boyhood dog, Rover, to my adulthood cat, Eddie; the one who inspired me to look back into my past to understand better why we have become such companions in old age!

CONTENTS

Prelude | 9
Rover | 11
Black | 13
Yestermorn | 15
Wonder | 17
Firefly | 19
Day | 21
Boyhood | 23
Raspberry | 25
Water | 27
Elm | 29
War | 31
Roof | 33
Pond | 35
Television | 37
Barking | 39
Fence | 41
Sled | 43
Morning | 45
Dog | 47
Lane | 49
Stream | 51
Urge | 54

Dawning | 56
Flashback | 58
Blizzard | 60
Creek | 62
Thursday | 64
Childhood | 66
Darkness | 68
Hearth | 70
Wish | 72
Swing | 74
Roadside | 76
Window | 78
Tears | 80
School | 82
Porch | 84
Hiker | 86
Sleep | 88
Door | 90
Wilderness | 92
Stroll | 94
Pantry | 96
Cogitation | 98
Postlude | 100

PRELUDE

I HAVE BEEN PONDERING for quite a while the theme of this book; not because of the hero of this book, but because of the animal that provoked me to think again of the childhood friend that started this love affair with a treasured pet. That pet today is a cat named Eddie who has already his own book (Meows from the Manse- not yet finished because Eddie is still alive). For most of my life I haven't been a great pet owner. I can honestly say I have never sought a pet, but dogs like Rover and cats like Eddie really do chose you. Eddie came one day as a stray, but Rover was the family dog that chose me to be his best friend. I believe it was because my father didn't have time for a dog in the busyness of being a dairy and potato farmer: a 24/7 kind of job. My mother didn't have time either, but unlike Dad never cared for any animal I know of. My sister Sylvia was Rover's other hope and though she paid a bit of attention to him she never has cared for animals that much. Granted, there were plenty of cousins and aunts and uncles and grandparents on the farm but they all seemed to have their own pets, so that left it for Rover to choose me. As I ponder on this boyhood friend nearly sixty years after Rover's passing, I have come to some conclusions and some remembrances.

It was the wise man Solomon who first wrote of " **. . . a friend that sticketh closer than a brother.**" (Proverbs 18:24) I have for most of my life read this as speaking of a human friend like my best friend Bob, a cousin, but a brother. As a pastor I have used this verse often to speak of the Lord Jesus Christ because He invoked this concept in His relationship to his disciples: **"Ye are my friends . . . "** (John 15:14) But as I study more the context of Solomon's proverb, I was directed to this concept also from pen of the mighty king of Israel: **"A righteous man regardeth the life of**

PRELUDE

his beast . . . " (Proverbs 12:10) Did Solomon have a pet? Often I have found in my mediations that sometimes it is the creature that gives more comfort and encouragement than the human. I can't tell you (you ought to read my 'Eddie' book) how much I have learned from Eddie and how much that simple feline has helped me through the years we have been together. It was the realization about Eddie that made me think back to Rover and what I might remember and reminisce about our relationship when I was a lad on the land. Before you are the stories I remember, and the lessons I now understand through a part German/Collie halfbreed becoming my boyhood friend. Come back with me into the late 1950s and early 1960s as my friend and I roam my ancestral homestead in search of adventure.

Also before you are the spiritual sermons Rover preached to me and the practical precepts I learned from a barnyard dog. I would only ever have one more dog in my life: a dog my wife and I called Cherry, during the early years of our marriage in Pembroke, New Hampshire. For these dog tales I am taking you back to Perham, Maine when the Blackstone homestead was still a working farm and dogs were a part of the animal zoo we had. Cows were for milking, pigs for meat, cats for moussing, and chickens for eggs, but Rover was just a "friend"; he wasn't even needed for guard duty in those days, days in which we "never" locked our doors (I don't think my parents ever knew were the keys to the house were). As I look back I realize that I had human friends, but my best friend was a dog we called Rover. So come with me back in time to a simpler age, a quiet time, a gentle period when a boy and his dog could walk together down country lanes together, and now I realize I still can walk with Rover again down memory lane!

Barry Blackstone—January 1, 2017

ROVER

WHEN YOU LIVE ON a potato and dairy farm for nearly twenty years, you come to enjoy harvesting, long summer evenings in the hay field, and the companionship of a dog. Though there were many dogs on the homestead in my boyhood, Rover was the most memorable of them all. Lady and Lassie come to mind, but Rover lives on in the sweet memory of a boy's best friend!

The intimacy I had with that dog goes back to some of the earliest of my childhood reflections. I can't remember when we got Rover, for he always seemed to be there in every boyhood MEMORY. I still see in my mind's eye, half-scrambling, half-leaping upon his back in the middle of the kitchen floor. At other times, I see myself laying peacefully beside him next to the big register in the living room. My first reflection of him is walking together beside the small stream that crossed the road just above the house. As I threw rocks into the water, Rover would bark with very splash. I can still see him impatiently setting in front of the chicken coop door wanting to come in, but not being allowed too. Rover was everybody's dog, but deep down I imagined him to be my dog, despite the fact he would walk with my sister Sylvia, and play with my cousin Clayton. Rover liked Dad and was often found with him in the barn.

Whether he was running after cats, or romping through the fields, Rover's favorite season was summer. Summer was filled with more places to go, and more activities for a farm dog. Winter was more of a vacation to the corner of the kitchen. I don't ever remember Rover liking the cold. Mother would never allow a cat into her house, but Rover must have won her heart. I see Rover now running through the tall grass on a warm summer day trying to catch butterflies, or grasshoppers. Rover chased anything that moved, even automobiles. We tried to break him of the bad habit, but we never did. He was one of the few dogs who managed to live to a grand old life without making a fatal mistake, though once I remember he came tragically close.

Rover was always caught up in the fragrance of the farm. With the nose being one of a dog's great senses, Rover was constantly sniffing out something. He loved to sniff out groundhogs in the pasture. He tracked rabbits in the woods. A cat couldn't come within a mile of his sensitive nose that he wouldn't be on the trail. I must have had an odor as well, for he always seemed to be able to find me even when I was hiding in a mount of hay. I think he like the challenge, for his nostrils were always moving in search of his next prey. Even when fall would come and the smells of summer changed, Rover kept up his pursuit of alien creatures invading his territory that is until the first snow can down. Then and only then would Rover retreat to the pantry or kitchen, where no doubt he slept dreaming of the smells of spring! These are just some of the things I remember of a boyhood, barnyard, backyard dog. My Dad taught me very early this concept from the pen of Job: **"But ask now the beasts, and they shall teach thee . . . Who knoweth not in all these that the hand of the Lord hath wrought this? In whose hand is the soul of every living thing (including dogs), and the breath of all mankind."** (Job 12:7, 9-10)

In my boyhood I never looked to Rover to teach me anything, if anything I tried to teach him a few dog tricks. Despite the fact my father pointed out this precept in Job in my youth, it has not been until adulthood that I have applied this principle to Eddie, my cat. It is now time to ask Rover again what instruction he was trying to share with me in the encounters and experiences we share in the boyhood of my youth!

BLACK

It is a dark, black day on the coast of Maine. It is Friday, a writing day for me. As a late fall storm blackens the sky outside my office at the Emmanuel Baptist Church of Ellsworth, Maine, I am pondering again my boyhood of the 1950's and 1960's. I've written in the past of my favorite color (green), and though black is not one of my favorites or so I thought; it is a color that brings back many a fond memory. I would like to share a few of the 'black' imagines I still have in the color corner of my cranial!

Black (his "**. . . visage is blacker than a coal . . .**"—Lamentations 4:8) was the color of my favorite dog. Rover was his name. A mixture of collie and German/shepherd, Rover was a midnight black. I have written of him often in my memories (I have compiled nearly 900 boyhood memories in a collection I call "Blackstone Homestead Memories"), but have thought of him more often in the last month than for a long time. My wife and I have been dog sitting a black cocker spaniel of some friends of ours as they have been vacationing in Florida. 'Nicky' is a nice dog, but she is no Rover. Rover was an once-in-a-lifetime dog. Maybe, it was because he was my first and only boyhood dog worth remembering, so over the years Rover has been exalted into the Dog's Hall of Fame, at least in my mind. We were walking 'Nicky' the other night and I said to my wife, Coleen, "Rover never had a leash." Rover was a free spirit, and so was I. As I ponder Rover this morning with my cat Eddie sleeping on a bookshelf in front of my desk it hit me; that the reason Eddie is so dear to me is the fact he has the spirit of Rover: loyal and free and he even has a little of Rover's black on his back!

Black was the color of the cows on the farm. We had a pure Holstein herd and the dominate colors of these creatures are black/

white. I can still see in my mind's eye between thirty and forty black and white cows grazing in a pasture of spring green. The black color of these animals caused them to stand out whether in the brown of fall or the white of winter just like Rover. The cows were a lot of work, but ever since the farm shut down its dairy, I have missed seeing this Blackstone black in the meadows with Rover.

Black was my father's favorite color, or so I thought. In my early childhood I don't remember we ever having a car that wasn't black. Most of the pictures of my sister Sylvia and me as infants were taken near a black car. Whether or not black was Dad's favorite color, you'll have to ask him in heaven for he passed into glory during the writing of this book, as for me I only remember black as his color. What I also seemingly remember is the time the color of our car changed. It was the mid-sixties and it was time for a new car. I think Dad wanted another black car, but mother insisted on a red car. How strange it seemed to me then, when the car dealer drove into the potato field behind the tool shed and said, "Here is your new car!" It was red on the outside, but if my memory serves me correctly it was black on the inside, the color of Rover!

Black was also the color of the letters on the potato barrels. Each fall the Blackstone homestead would erupt in a fury of activity. The annual potato harvest was upon us, and there was much preparation. One of the things I remember doing was stenciling the letters B-L-A-C-K-S-T-O-N-E on the sides of all our barrels. Some only had to be redone, but the new barrels all had to have those letters painted on their side. For me, those black letters were a source of pride. And as I can see from this article, black was really and still is a favorite color of mine, a Blackstone black as seen in the fur of a dog! Jesus is recorded as saying in His famous sermon: **"Neither shalt thou swear by thy head, because thou canst not make one hair white or black."** (Matthew 5:36)

YESTERMORN

A TEN-YEAR OLD BOY stood silently gazing out a second story window to the road that ran through the Sugar Woods (the forest that separates the two halves of the Blackstone homestead). A herd of black and white cows were grazing lazily in the pasture just cross the barnyard. But neither the path nor the pasture caught the boy's eye that particular morning; he merely stood and stared ahead, seeing with his mind rather than his eye the stream that lay on the other side of the ridge. He had climbed the flight of stairs in the middle of the rambling farmhouse to his corner bedroom to change his cloths for hiking. As he stared out the window in introspection, his mind returned to the stream that ran through his hometown of Perham, Maine, especially the section which flowed through Bragdon's (next door neighbors of the Blackstones since 1861) back field. It was a favorite place, even though it was a two mile walk one way that is if he stayed to the main road. If he cut across the back field and through the woods, it was a lot shorter. It was a beautiful day for a hike, and with his barn chores done, he would go!

He stood and stared a few more moments, then turned and left his room. He quietly descended the stairs until he reached the main floor of the old house his grandfather had bought for his parents in the late 1940's. The boy left the house through the front door that opened to a huge porch that ran the entire length of the home. Climbing down the porch steps, the wanderer headed down the grassy incline that lead to the path which would take him to the Russell Place (a series of fields bought with the house and barn from a family called Russell). By the time he made the pasture his favorite boyhood friend, a dog called Rover joined him. Even as they left the yard, he could hear the distant sounds of the forest that lay between him and his special brook. As they neared the woods behind his father's cow barn, the sounds of nature grew louder and louder. On many a day he had played with his Blackstone cousins and the McDougal boys (neighbors) in the same forest lane, but today he wanted to be alone with his dog on this adventure to Salmon Brook. For on this day of contemplation, the lad wanted only the voices of field and forest, stream and sparrow and his best friend to interrupt his thoughts.

Twenty minutes later the boy and dog were crossing the lower end of the pasture just below the milking shed (where the Blackstone milked their cows in the summer). They made their way up the small hill to an orchard he had often hunted partridge in, just behind the Dickinson Homestead. He and his cousins had often taken the same route checking the fence line, or cutting the tall grass that often shorted out the electric fence that keep the Holstein herd in the pasture. But today, they bypassed the pasture and orchard in favor of the beckoning brook on the other side of the woods. Turning right, they walked the length of a hay field owned by the Bragdon's, before once again entering the woods by way of a field road that lead down to the stream. It seemed whenever his mind turned serious; Rover would focus him back to the sound of the stream before him.

With the pleasant memory of a stream and a dog still fresh in my mind, I end these thoughts of a yestermorn with this Biblical challenge: **"The memory of the just is blessed . . . "** (Proverbs 10:7) Is there a more precious asset than a good memory? As I compile this series of articles in which my boyhood dog Rover is at the heart of each chapter, I am battling the reality that my father has lost most of his mind with dementia. As he nears 93, his mind is just about gone (and his life left him on February 7, 2017), but it amazes me just how many memories he had left. That is why I write, lest I forget these precious memories with my dog Rover.

WONDER

IN THE ADVANCEMENTS OF mankind, we have lost something irreplaceable: the wonder of life. With the urbanization of the city swallowing up the utopia of the country, we have lost the simple awe and quiet inspiration that comes from walking along a brook with a dog, working in a barnyard beside a Rover, and whistling with a bird as your 'best friend' barks in unison. With our over dependence on technology, we have lost the excitement that comes from living on a farm and in a field, on a hill and in a hollow (my boyhood home was located in a hollow). Today most people are surrounded with traffic not trees, streets not streams. Their only stimulation comes from the manipulative media who glorifies the glitter and glamour of urban life verses country life. Malls have replaced meadows, neon lights have replaced night lights, and the telescope has been replaced by the television. Unless it is video or VCR, people rarely wonder at the sights they are seeing, and there is still something wonderful about a dog without a leash!

I am thankful for the wonder of a boyhood with a dog. On my family farm in the 1950's and 1960's I had a childhood and a dog. Today before most boys are teenagers they have become old and aged, critical and cynical and that happens without a dog. They have been robbed of "The Wonder Years" by the sensual, sinful and sordid society they live in. As for me, I lived in the sweet solitude of a rural ranch isolated by distance and dignity with a dog. No perverts there to prey on the innocent, just wonderful examples of manhood (On my visit to Perham for my father's funeral I met again one of those men-Woody Doody, my little league coach now 85 but still a 'gentle' man) and womanhood, whether family or friend, teacher or preacher. No pimps there to plunder the purity of boys, just helpful bus drivers and janitors, coaches and church leaders and a dog to play with and be protected by. No wonder I had wished that my children had grown up a bit slower (I think this today again as I watch my 39-year old die of cancer), for I fear they lost the wonder of childhood even though I tried to teach them 'the wonder of it all' without a dog; they had plenty of pets but no dog, no dog like Rover and I see the results today, especially in my son.

I am thankful for the wonder of a backyard. For most a backyard is only a few feet of lawn between their house and their neighbor's garage; so it is with me now, but once upon a time I had a backyard behind my barnyard; acres of pastureland and woodland to roam with my dog, and to call home. My lot wasn't to escape into the "tube", but into the trees. My world wasn't a fantasy of mechanical gadgets and technological games, but of forest and field. For most kids today the backyard is the backroom and a Nintendo. Hemmed in by walls, their minds can't develop properly the ability to wonder. Granted, the modern day child can handle the control mechanism of a video game with exceptional speed and dexterity, but they soon get lost in the real world. I learned little of Mario, but the mysteries and the majesty of lakes and larks I learned to wonder at through the companionship of a dog. I simply ask: **"Which uplifts most?"** Who is really in touch with life? Where is inspiration in this? No wonder we have a generation so deep in despair; they need a dog; the time saving and tremendous help of our inventions does not compensate us for the stress and strain they add to our life and lifestyle and living.

The tragedy today is that most wander, not wonder. That is why a backyard with a dog is so important! I believe the psalmist hit the nail on the head when he said: **"Our fathers understood not thy wonder in Egypt . . . "** (Psalm 106:7) If the people of Moses' day had missed the wonders of the plagues and the miracles of the wilderness wandering than it is not hard to believe the 'wonders' we are missing today. You know by now I am of the belief that part of the problem is that not enough people have a pet like Rover or Eddie!

FIREFLY

IT IS MID-JULY ON the coast of Maine, and last night was one of those perfect "mid-summer night" evenings; not hot nor humid, but warm and pleasant with just enough breeze to refresh you both physically and spiritually. It is on a night like that I reflect on a similar time when I was a boy with my dog Rover on a farm in Northern Maine. Rarely did the sticky humidity of the south reach that far north, and one could almost guarantee that once the sun began to set the air would begin to cool no matter the daytime temperature before it. As dusk turned into darkness and blackness invaded the barnyard another enjoyable event took place around the family home: the flight of the fireflies and their effect on me and my dog Rover.

It wasn't until years later that I learned much about what we were enjoying and who we were dancing with. During those carefree days of my youth all I cared about was catching fireflies in a bottle. Chasing fireflies through the tall grass by the potato house was a summer adventure remembered fondly. My dog and I spend a good many warm summer's eve in search of what we called "lighting bugs".

According to the Expects, the flashing lights that attracted my dog and I was in actuality a chemical reaction taking place. Bioluminescence is the scientific name given to the process. I have learned that there are nearly 2000 kinds of fireflies and that each one has its own light code (what a wonderful Creator we believe in). I was saddened to learn that they were not flashing their lights for Rover or me. The flicker of light from their abdomen was for attracting a mate. A firefly will set on the stem of a high blade of field grass and wait for another firefly to pass. If the correct light is flashed and returned, there is a match! Little did I imagine what

FIREFLY

I was interrupting on those warm summer evening on the Blackstone Homestead when Rover and I went about chasing 'lights'?

Another favorite hunting ground for fireflies for my dog and I was across the road from our home. A small field boxed in by woods always had an abundance of these beetle-like creatures. Feeding during the day on pollen, the "glowworm" as he is sometimes called, would only reveal himself when dusk could reflect the glow of his light. Grabbing an old canning jar, I would set out to catch enough fireflies to make my own flashlight. Easier said than done, the firefly would resist capture by moving between flashes, for it was only during that tiny spark that the fly was vulnerable. I caught a few, but I was never a great firefly catcher and neither was Rover. I was also to compassionate to be very good at it. I can't remember ever keeping any of them. After we tired of running around, we would always let them go. Periodically, we might take them home to show Mom and Dad, but before we were off to bed, they were released into the backyard!

I live in the city now with few fireflies ever being seen in my backyard. It is for this reason I must chase fireflies in my mind and memory; see again only in my memory a field sparking with thousands of tiny lights inviting me and my dog to a dance. The sun sets and the frogs begin their croaking from the pond across the way, and Rover and I are lead to a field by a spark in the dark! I don't know about you but I have always been amazed at the simplicity in the diversity that the Great Creator God put in His creation. As He created " . . . the lesser light to rule the night . . . " (Genesis 1:16) on the 4th day of creation; He also created a tiny " . . . creeping thing . . . " (Genesis 1:24), not to rule the night on the 6th day, but to light the night for a boy and his boyhood friend that they might have a wonderful time of play in the dusk of their relationship with a few fireflies.

DAY

THERE IS NOTHING LIKE a day spent in the country. After spending a day like I have today in the city, I long for one more chance to experience a day in my childhood. When I was younger I wished the best days of my life away. So as I set at my desk at the Emmanuel Baptist Church in Ellsworth, Maine, my only relief from this hurried city day is to return in my mind to the pleasant 'dog days of summer'.

It was hot and humid in the city this morning, but in my country home in Perham, Maine the morning's coolness is now fondly remembered. Long before the sun began its daily trip over my family's homestead, the course of my day had already been set. There were early morning chores, and the aroma of a cow barn in the early morning is still one of my favorite smells, including the manure. Returning to the old farm house brought another smell to my nostrils. Near the back door was Mom's flower garden. As I crossed the short distance between the house and the barn the aromas of the surrounding trees in full spring bloom and Mother's perennials created a combination of smells unmatched by any botanical garden, and of course following every step of the way was my dog Rover!

After a hardy breakfast, it was back into the freshness of a Maine Day on the farm. No matter how high or hot the sun would get, there always seemed to be a gusty breeze to cool me down. As I went from spot to spot on the farm with my trusted friend by my side, doing whatever needed to be done, I was constantly confronted with the colors of creation. I remember bright-winged butterflies fluttering about, and green grasshoppers jumping about and with every moving insect Ross would either chasing them or snapping at them. I saw multi-colored apple blossoms hanging from the orchard, and big brown bugs hanging from the trees. I see white fluffy cloud floating over head against a brilliant blue sky. I walked in green and white pastures filled with clover watching black and white Holsteins grazing. Periodically, birds of ever shape and size and color would draw my attention skyward again. Pink pigs, cream cats, dark dogs, and rust colored roasters could also be found on the homestead on a typical day. But the best color of all was the black velvet of my faithful companion Rover!

As a day on the homestead neared its end, the air turned cold, and the stars began to appear in the open canvas above. It was then we often went out to the porch for nature's grand show. Add to the lighting of moonshine and star shine and fireflies, the soprano of the sparrows, the tenor of the crickets, the melody of Rover my dog, and the bass of the bull frogs in a nearby pond, and you had the background music for our night's entertainment. Against this quartet was the hum of the wind blowing through the trees that surrounded our home. Though we were often joined by millers and moths and an assortment of other bugs attracted by the porch light, we didn't seem to mind them as we relaxed from a hard day's work, reflecting on the beauty of the day, and the wonder of living it with a country dog for another day!

What is so nice about remembering such days in my boyhood was the spiritual lesson I was taught very early in my life. I can't remember if it was my father, my mother, my grandparents or my Sunday school teacher that first pointed out this classic concept from the Psalms: **"This is the day which the Lord has made; we will rejoice and be glad in it."** (Psalm 118:24) Each day, every day was a day from the Almighty and we were to rejoice in each of them. What I like best about memory is the fact that a boyhood day spent with your dog can be relived and instead of rejoicing in it once it can be rejoiced in again and again!

BOYHOOD

I REMEMBER MY BOYHOOD for its independence of movement. I was allowed to roam freely throughout the farm with Rover at my side. I rarely remember being asked by my parents, "Where are you going?" Or, "Who will you be playing with today?" When you live on a back road farm in northern Maine, there were few options, so my parents were relaxed disciplinarians who gave me much latitude. With money always scares, there were few toys, but Rover and I had great imaginations!

Around chores, we had plenty of time for fun. We played basketball in the cow barn, on our own court; Rover loved any ball, especially a moving ball. We played baseball against the front of the huge barn that sat beside our old farm house. We went swimming in the frog pond in the cow pasture. We went fishing in the stream that ran long the backside of the homestead's northern boundary. There were wars to be fought in the woods against an invading German force, and Indian uprising to be put down in the forts of the haymow. Needless to say, I had a very active boyhood with few physical shortcomings to interrupt my almost daily adventures. The only exceptions I can remember was a rare case of Ring Worm I contracted from my Grandfather Blackstone and a trip to the hospital to get my tonsils out. Other than those setbacks, my boyhood wealth was in my boyhood health and the companionship of a great dog named Rover!

As the years passed, I grew steadily. I was always proud I was the tallest, if not the biggest of my Blackstone cousins. The McDougal's, our only real neighbors, had plenty of boys, but once again they were small in stature. I was athletic and skillful in all Perham sports. I was a Perham Pirate, the local Little League Team, and played a lot, even when I was nine. We had a great coach in

BOYHOOD

Woody Doody, the meat cutter at Holt's General Store, and at eleven, we won the district championship over the bigger towns of Washburn, Wade, Woodland, and Crouseville. In the school yard games, I excelled, whether in snow football, or tag. I was tall and lanky, and competitive. I still feel the joy of running through a sea of classmates for a touchdown, or going six for six against our rivals at the Woodland Elementary School in our annual baseball game. Before I reached high school, I had grown to 5' 10", and was a freshman starter on the Washburn varsity baseball team. (I reached my teenage years, but Rover never did!)

Rover and I loved the four seasons, for with each came something different to do. We got bored easily, so with the variety of work on the farm, and the variety of activities at school, there was always a change in the routine. We loved spring for dam making and tossing a baseball. We loved summer for haying and our annual trip to Dinsmore's Camp on Madawaska Lake for horseshoes. I loved fall for throwing the grapples during potato harvest and for hunting partridge. I loved winter for its snow storms and playing basketball. As I look back, I realize that I was one of those fortunate lads who had a great boyhood with a dog! I don't know if Jesus had a dog, but I have been teaching young people for years that one of the reasons we can believe in Jesus Christ is the fact He knew about being a kid. Whichever age you are at, He knows about being five and twelve and seventeen. Luke tells us this about the boyhood of Jesus: "And the child grew, and waxed strong in spirit, filled with wisdom: and the grace of God was upon him . . . And Jesus increased in wisdom and stature, and in favour with God and man." (Luke 2:40, 52) Over the years I have been able to relate to Jesus because His boyhood in Nazareth was much like my boyhood in Perham with the exception of Rover, or was it?

RASPBERRY

I AM RECORDING THESE memories of my beloved, boyhood, dog Rover in the midst of a heavy wet snow storm in the middle of a March blizzard in Maine. I do not know the reason one's mind skips seasons, but for me I suddenly was again on my family's farm in Perham, Maine picking raspberries with my dog Rover; not your typical cultivated raspberries, but wild raspberries. The thing that makes this memory so strange is that I don't even like raspberries, but what I liked was to pick raspberries with Rover.

It is late July somewhere in the early 1960's. It's hot, very hot and muggy. Dad would say: "good haying weather", but on this particular morning I would work for Mum not Dad. To beat the heat I tell Mother I would go and pick her some raspberries for lunch. She loved raspberries and I knew just the spot to find them in abundance; big, bright, beautiful ones, and I also knew the perfect companion to go with.

As I made my way through the woods towards the Salmon Lake Road with Rover by my side, I felt better already. Walking in the woods with a dog is the surest way I know to cool off on a steamy summer's day. The gentle breeze through the cooler trees is nature's natural air conditioner, and if you live in the city like I do now, man has yet to come up with an adequate substitute, in my opinion. As we emerged from the forest about a half a mile up the road we headed straight for the rock and tree line that separated our farm from Abel Brissette's land. Along that hedgerow grew the biggest wild raspberries I have ever seen. Maine Black Bears, and I'm not talking about hockey players, often feasted along that hedge. They know where to find fine dining in Perham. To my knowledge there was only one other place better than this for

RASPBERRY

raspberries, and that was also on my Father's farm; another place only known to Rover and me.

As I moved into the raspberry bushes I found the canes were loaded with berries. The weight of the fruit had bowed the canes to my knees. As I picked, I moved slowly through the harvest before me. Moving a scrawny bush aside, I discovered an inconspicuous cane bent very low in the back. When I lifted it up I found on its underside no less than twenty-five ripe raspberries. But they were not your ordinary raspberries. All I could think of was that cluster of grapes the twelve Hebrew spies brought back after their exploration of Canaan: **"And they came unto the brook of Eschol, and cut down from thence a branch with one cluster of grapes, and they bare it between two upon a staff . . . ."** (Numbers 13:21) Isn't it funny how a Sunday school lesson and a trip to get berries for your mother merge? I knew nobody would believe me, but through I couldn't bring back the branch I could bring back the berries. As I took them from their home one at a time I marveled at their size, and then my eye fell upon the raspberry of all raspberries. Tucked away at the very end was the granddaddy of them all. It was bigger than my thumb; now that's a raspberry!

After I picked several quarts of these wonderful, perfect berries, Rover and I headed home for lunch. For dessert that day I enjoyed watching my family add sugar and cream to my morning's harvest. Though I didn't enjoy eating any of them myself, I still thought and think to this day I got the best end of that experience, the better of the deal. Berries and blizzards do go together, just like boys and dogs! The sermon is clear to me: anything you do is more pleasant with a companion. Like me, Rover didn't like raspberries, so the more we picked the more ended up in the jar instead of in our mouth. More for the family than more for me: **"Look not every man on his own things . . . "** (Philippians 2:4)

WATER

"Still waters" don't have to be big waters like David talked about in his world-famous psalm: "**. . . He leadeth me beside still waters.**" (Psalm 23:2). Granted, I have spent more time near brooks and rivers and creeks and streams, but my first experience with 'still waters' were the springs on my father's farm with my dog Rover.

I loved as a child to walk through the cow pastures in search of groundhogs, and so did Rover. Dad had given me permission to kill every groundhog, better known as woodchuck, I could find. Their holes could break a cow's leg, so they were a danger to the Holstein herd. On my adventures after the crafty woodchuck, Rover and I would often discover a spring near their burrows. On a warm afternoon, we would quench our thirst from the small streams draining from the rocky ledge. It was then I fell in love with spring water. There is no water on earth as sweet as water from granite. Once I located these special water sources, I would repeatedly return. Whether hunting or harvesting, picking rocks or picking mustard (a weed), rare was the time I came close to those springs that I didn't stop by for a taste and a touch. Water from a rock will quench your thirst like no other water, just ask Rover; because he loved the refreshing taste just like me and would lap up as much as he could before following me on to our next adventure!

Something else I learned by these springs of water was that they were also excellent places for meditation. The sound of bubbling water out of the ground is one of the calming noises in the world (like walking along a sea edge on a beach on the Jersey shore like I am doing on the day of this writing). These constant streams of water generate a simple sound that provokes thought.

WATER

One of my favorite springs was located in a pasture just below our old milking shed. Resting on a small hillside, the spring also overlooked a number of groundhog holes nearby. Often Rover and I would set by this spring watching for any woodchuck crazy enough to venture out of its burrow. We sat there hour after hour in my boyhood, and now I wonder if it wasn't more for the mediation than for murder. It was an airy spot that was not only beautiful, but abounding with things to see. Beyond the pasture was a huge field (now owned by an Amish man named Eli) that was either blooming with potato blossoms, or filling the air with sweet clover, or yellow with ripening grain. Behind were the Sugar Woods, where the family had tapped trees for their sweet syrup. In front of me was a small pond that no doubt the spring helped to fill. It was a quiet spot that provoked thought and mediation, and now I see, memory. This kind of water quenches your thirst in more ways than one.

I remember well the woodchucks I wounded there, and the groundhogs I killed there, but I best remember the sweet hours of serenity Rover and I spent there. I also best remember the gallons of pure, clear water we drank there, and the countless breaks we enjoyed there. I never remember a 'coffee break' on the farm, but I happily recall the times dad would say after we finished a trip through the field picking rocks in the heat of a June afternoon, **"Let's walk down to the spring and get a drink!"** How far that water had travelled underground I know not, but its sweet taste will never, ever be forgotten, for it was water with a friend. I know not if David had a 'sheep-dog' to help him in caring for his father's flock (I Samuel 16:11), but I do know David must have known the places on the family homestead where he could take the sheep for a drink. Every day, maybe twice a day or more, David would have to lead the flock to water. As the sheep drank, what do you think David did? I believe he mediated and in those mediations he no doubt wrote some of his beloved psalms including the one that has inspired this chapter on Rover. Sitting by a bubbling spring and rubbing a dog's head are great moments for mediation!

ELM

As a boy in northern Maine during the 1950's and 1960's, I lived on my family's ancestral homestead whose history could be traced back to the year of 1861 and my great-great-great grandfather Hartson. On the front lawn of the original home (the first framed house ever built in Perham, Maine) of that farm once grew a stately elm tree. Whether it was planted there, or was there when the house was built nobody in my family seems to know, but what memories I have of that ancient tree and my dog 'Rover'.

When I was a child that old elm had reached its zenith in life, probably nearing the grand old age of 150? The roots of that tree were massive reaching well beyond the limit of its shade. Its branches not only gave shade to the lawn, but the Blackstone Road that ran right beside it. Its position on the lawn was the highlight of a circular driveway. I remember mowing the lawn and having to push the lawn mower over the roots that ran above the ground in places. Its trunk could only be hugged if my cousins and I locked hands around it with Rover, paw to tail. Despite its wide base, it soon branched out only a few feet above the ground. This made it easy for me and my cousins to get into its top. It was a great place to hide behind in a game of 'kick the can', and it was a great place to defend in a game of 'war'! It was usually the starting place for the child to count during a game of 'hide and seek'. Its limbs and its branches provided wonderful places for ambush during a game of 'Cowboys and Indians' and 'Rin Tin Tin', the part Rover always played!

It had three huge limbs growing upward and outward. Its tallest twig reached well above the height of the two story farm house. Only the large cow barn stood above it in the barnyard. I can still see all the different size potato baskets lined up under its

ELM

branches just before autumn's harvest. It was tall enough to park trucks loaded down with hay under, as well as farm machinery of all shapes and sizes. It was a wind break in the winter and a cooling shade tree in the summer. It was a resting place between loads of hay, and a contemplation place when you needed to think. It was a waiting place before your ride to the potato field arrived, and it was a story-telling place for Gramp.

It had cows and horses tied to it, and if my memory serves me correctly, a cousin or two as well, but never a dog because I never, ever remember Rover on a leash! If that elm could have only recorded what took place under its shadow what a story it could tell, and what tales it could have told about Rover?

Of course, as I write this remembrance about Rover and my childhood elm, the tree is dead and so is Rover. Its mighty branches and massive base were cut and pulled from the ground years ago because it had become a danger. All that remains are the ugly roots that still in places emerge from the front lawn. There is really nothing that remains to tell you of its grand estate that is except in my memory. Time and wind and disease eventually took its toll on this solitary sentinel on Blackstone Road. It has gone the way of the farmstead and Rover; still alive in memory, but dead. It had a slow, agonizing dying as I see it. Like the homestead, the root structure is still spread out, but with no nourishment from above, the roots die with the land, but in one place both elm and farm and Rover are alive and well, and that is in the remembrances of this homesteader who lived in the shade of that mighty elm and that marvelous estate with a dog called 'Rover'.

The elm is a Biblical tree (Hosea 4:13—" . . . **under oaks and poplars and elms, because the shadow thereof is good . . .** ") as well as a Blackstone tree, but most importantly it is a boyhood tree. Another reminder that helps me recall the grand times I had with Rover!

WAR

APPLE SEASON HAS COME again to Maine (every fall one of the joys my wife Coleen and I share is picking our annual store of apples from the local apple orchard here in Ellsworth), and with it a memory of the great homestead apple 'wars' my cousins and I and my 'war dog' Rover use to wage in the various orchards scattered around the farm.

Still to this day around the Blackstone Homestead in Perham, Maine is a series of apple orchards. I discovered recently the source of one of these orchards when I read this in the obituary of Eben Fremont Blackstone, a great-great uncle! Eben was the third son of Hartson and Ruth Blackstone, the original pioneers of the Blackstone farm:

"Coming as he did from an apple growing country, one of Mr. Blackstone's first efforts at farming was the planting of six crab apple trees which he carried through the woods from Westfield. (Interestingly, a town I had a pastorate in between 1978-1986!) Later in life Mr. Blackstone's orchard was his hobby. The day before his death he walked through his orchard and admired the wealth of pink buds just bursting into bloom. He was especially interested in sweet apples and had a few fine Monroe trees which were his pride."

Immediately across the road from where I lived was an old set of farm buildings, including a two story house and a leaning barn. The barn was in such poor shape that it was only used to keep things undercover. Behind that falling down barn was an orchard of about 20 trees. It was not the orchard Uncle Eben planted because it was a part of a farm (The Russell Place) my grandfather brought in the late 1940's, but it did have its share of crab apple trees. On a day when there was little going on, my cousins, a few of the local neighbor's kids, and I, and of course Rover who never missed an apple fight, would gather in the old orchard for an afternoon of warfare. We were always playing Cowboys and Indians or war games, but when the apple trees began to produce, we went from imaginary ammo to 'apple bullets'; how Rover loved to pick apples from the ground and place them in my hand, but his throwing was terrible!

Filling our pockets full of the small apples, we would then pick armies. Often, one army would defend the old fort (the barn) while the other army would attack. Strategy was to see who could hit all the other soldiers before all your soldiers were hit. It was not a war for the faint of heart, for if you have ever been hit with a crabapple it was not a pain-less wound. The war usually began with an opening salvo by the attacking platoon. Those behind defensive position (cow stalls or grain bens) usually fared pretty well until their fox holes were out flanked (Rover proved to be a wonderful sentry in such situations), or overrun. Close apple to apple fighting came when those not 'appled' (my word) were surrounded. The war ended when all were 'hit' or the apple supply ran out. The advantage to the attacking team was they still could make an 'ammo apple' run to the orchard while the defending army had to depend on used apples, or their hoard of apples.

There were always a few tears and pleads for mercy, but over the years I never remember a call for a 'no more crab apple war' peace treaty! Peace only lasted as long as it took to get another load of crab apples, to carry the hurting home, to choose up sides again, and to hear Rover's bark that began the flight of apples all over again! When Jesus spoke of " . . . **wars and rumors of wars** . . . " (Matthew 24:6) I know he wasn't taking about 'crabapple wars', but whether a real war or a pretend war, warfare is a reality of the world we live in even in one's boyhood. I for one am looking for the day when "they will practice war no more" even if that means Rover won't be a part of the peace treaty!

ROOF

LAST NIGHT I WAS watching a concert on PBS (Public Broadcasting Station of Maine) by James Taylor. I must admit I have been listening to this man's music since the 1960's, but I never saw him before last night. I thought he was a black man! As he played and sang the old songs I remember from my boyhood, he was nearing the end of a set when he sang the classic 60s song, "Up on the Roof". You know the one that starts, "When this old world is getting you down . . . " Despite the fact he was singing of a roof " . . . in the midst of town . . . " I was carried back to the top of a roof in the county of my birth and the sounds of my barking dog Rover could be heard echoing off the side of our massive cow barn.

Like any farm boy, I loved to climb. Even to this day I am not afraid of heights. If it was off the floor or off the ground I liked to be there. (A practice my twenty-one month grandson Judah has taken up with a passion!) At first, I tackled the easy climbs, like the wood pile and the clothesline. Then it was higher heights, like the spruce tree in the front lawn, and the beams in the haymow. Even when at work on the farm climbing was often connected to our labor. My record climb in that category was at the end of a 40 foot extension ladder, extended, on a platform built on the top of side panels on the back of the farm truck. My destination was the peak of the cow barn. My mission was to paint that peak. I accomplished that task on the cow barns, both back and front. (Just last week my Cousin Dale was down to pay his respects at the passing of my son Scott and he reminded me of the first time I made that climb and the gallon of pain I dumped on his head!) Despite the height, it was not my greatest climb on the homestead; the greatest was for pure pleasure.

ROOF

The cow barn near my home, though not as large as the main cow barn, was just as high. It was even higher off the back end where its height also included the depth of the cellar. I loved that old barn. It was completely destroyed by fire after I left the farm, but remains clearly visible in my memory to this day. During my stay on the homestead that old barn offered many an adventures for me and Rover, and the ultimate had to have been the first time I climbed 'up on the roof' with Rover watching; not much of a climber!

It wasn't as difficult as you might think, unless you are afraid of heights. A rod iron ladder ran up the side of the barn, and along the three section roof. A typical Aroostook County barn, the old barn had about twenty foot walls then the rest of the barn was a pitched roof. The first section of roof was highly pitched, but the ladder gave you plenty of holding power. The second pitch wasn't as bad, and by the time you got to the third you could walk quite well. It was and still is the best roof I have ever been on. From the top of that roof you could see for miles, except on the side that pointed to Caribou. A high ridge blocked you vision in that direction, but the rest was spectacular. I can still see in my mind's eye the sights I saw as I sat on the peak of that roof. The Holsteins in the back pasture looked so small. Rover, my dog, was barking playfully in the driveway, but even his bark seemed a distant sound. My cousins, who had dared me into the climb in the first place, were yelling for me to be careful, but I was lost in the solitude of the altitude. I didn't know the song "Up on the Roof" then, but the author must have had a similar experience, for I too " . . . found a paradise so fresh and clear, up on the roof!"

My favorite 'roof' story in the Bible is about four friends who had a cripple friend (Mark 2:1-11) that needed a healing. When they got to the place that Jesus was preaching they discovered he was in a house and the crowd was so large the house was full and the yard was full. Instead of trying to push their way through the crowd with their friend on a hand bed, they came up with a unique way of getting their friend to Jesus: they went up on the roof and made a big enough hole in the roof to lower the bed with their friend on it to the feet of Jesus. From up on the roof the four friends watched Jesus heal their friend!

POND

ONLY THE INDIVIDUAL WHO has spent a severe winter in a northern climate will understand fully the wonderful places of spring. I like snow, but I love the melting of snow better. The weatherman says that it will snow tonight. If it does it will be the first of the season. Not since late April have I seen snow. It is now the middle of December and we have yet to receive a lasting snowfall; a few flurries a couple of times but nothing that has stayed. I find it interesting as I begin my 31th winter on the coast of Maine that my mind is already into spring. As I am waiting for the cold weather to freeze my favorite ice fishing pond, I am actually today pondering on my boyhood dog's favorite pond.

On the farm of my boyhood where are a number of small ponds. Each was created by a spring and was used for watering the Holstein herd in various pastures located around the homestead. Dad also used the water source to spray the crops with. Though they had a practical use in the daily running of farm operations, they also played a vital part in the recreation enterprises of my dog and I. For us, they were not watering spots or spray holes, but ponds for swimming, playing, and creating naval battles!

There really was no other physical experience on the farm which quite matched the magic around these small bodies of water, especially the one directly across the road from my childhood home. Surrounded by small bushes and lined with reeds, this favorite pond wouldn't have measure more than thirty feet by thirty feet. Yet it drew us to its backs on many an occasion, and I wonder to this day how many time Rover went to that pond for a bath that I never knew about? Sometimes we went there too simply cool off from a very hot summer's day. Nothing is so designed to stimulate the entire body and quicken all the senses as to jump into a frog pond with all your clothes on in a streaming July afternoon. We cared no that we got our clothes or fur wet, for we knew that they would soon dry in the scorching sun. It was a refreshing plunge into spring water; mud and all! Oh, I forgot to tell you about the muddy water didn't I. Despite the fact that the small pond was feed from a spring, it was a dead pond. Meaning it had an inlet but no outlet. As the summer got hotter and hotter, the water in the pond got stale. Sometimes brown in color and oftentimes green would be its dominating reflection. No matter, we were there to catch frogs and to get cool and to have fun.

One of the last times Rover and I played in that pond will forever be remembered. We reenacted a naval battle on the surface of that small ocean. I made models of ships and enjoyed sinking them with cannon shot: small rocks or shot from my trusty bee-bee rifle! As we set the two opposing fleets adrift on the water, I would lob stones at them, or try to shot holes in their sides so they would sink, while Rover barked. How many naval vessels still lay buried at the bottom of that pond I cannot say, but I well remember the titanic struggle waged in the basin of that small pond as my dog and I would spend an afternoon sealing the fate of nations that to me made the Battle of Jutland and the Battle of Midway very real! I was the captain and Rover was my firstmate and we waged naval warfare together on the banks of our favorite homestead pond!

When I went to Israel in May of 2010 I had a chance to visit two of the most famous 'ponds' called pools in the Bible: the Pool of Bethesda (John 5:12) where the impotent man was healed and the Pool of Siloam (John 9:7) where the blind man was healed. What amazed me most as I walked around the archeological sites containing the old sites of these ponds was the simple fact they were no larger than my small pond on the farm.

TELEVISION

BELIEVE IT OR NOT, I grew up through the 1950's without a television in my homestead home! It wasn't that I didn't see a television, for my city grandfather (Barton) had one, and we use to visit. Friday was shopping day, and my mother and father and sister Sylvia (my other sister and two brothers didn't come along until we had our own television) and I use to travel the twenty miles to the big city of Presque Isle at least once a month to pick up things we couldn't get in our small village of Perham, Maine. It was in my grandfather's living room I fell in love with the television. (I still love television though I am getting tired with the change of content) I can still remember my sister and me pleading with our Dad to buy one of these modern instruments of entertainment. I think the reason I am reminded of those days is because we have become a VCR-less family again. Our old VCR finally died the other day, and ever since, my two kids have been asking when are we going to get a new one. Our old television is also on its last legs, so my wife and I have been checking prices for a new TV and VCR! The quest has taken me back in time and to a dog named Rover.

    Despite the appeal of the new technology, Dad knew we didn't have the money for a television. So for many years, my sister and I had to be content with our monthly trip to Gramp's house. Then when I was nine, Dad and Mum scrapped enough money together to buy a black and white television. I can still feel the excitement as the television was set up in a corner of our living room. My memory is that they bought it from a man by the name of Mr. Doak from Caribou. Mr. Doak had a television repair shop about fifteen miles from the homestead. Living in rural northern Maine, the only station we could pick up on the 'rabbit-ears' was Channel 8 out of Presque Isle; WAGM I believe. If my memory serves me

TELEVISION

well, at that time Channel 8 didn't even broadcast 24 hours a day, just some evening programs. The programming was limited, but one particular memory does overshadow them all!

When I was young, one of my favorite past times, when I did have time, was playing with my dog Rover. I believe I got that love from a television show called "Rin Tin Tin".

It was my favorite, boyhood show. I liked Rawhide, The Rifleman, Wagon Train, and The Lone Ranger, but "Rin Tin Tin" will always be my favorite childhood show, probably because it was my first western with a dog as the main character. I can still hear the music in my ear, and my mind's eye still sees 'Rinie' standing on a huge boulder barking for the cavalry to come to the rescue. I sat glued in front of the television until the show was over; until my television hero had captures the bad guys; until the pioneers were once again safe, and until Rinie had come to the rescue.

Often I would get so involved in the show that when the gunfight began I would pull out the six shooter from the holster at my side. Before I knew it my sister sitting across the room was the bad guy and Rover and I were in hot pursuit. Loading with caps, the living room at the Blackstone house would explode in gunfire. Seeing my hero on top of the bad guy, I would climb aboard my trusty footstool and with a last call to "Rin Tin Tin", Rinie (Rover) and I would ride off to the kitchen of a late night snack! The next day Rover and I would reenact the story line of the weekly television show in the barnyard and backyard of the homestead. To this day I still see in my mind those adventures in fantasy. How powerful is the eye: "The light of the body is the eye: if therefore thine eye be single, thy whole body shall be full of light." (Matthew 6:22) Even if your eye were on a television dog that materialized in a barnyard dog named Rover!

BARKING

When I was young, Old MacDonald's Farm was the Blackstone Farm in Perham, Maine, and my favorite barnyard sound was **"with a bow wow here and a bow wow there, here a bow there a bow everywhere a bow wow!"**

I yearn for that appealing sound again. At the present my wife and I are babysitting a dog of some friends of ours, but this dog doesn't bark! It doesn't yap, yelp, or yip either! I long again for a barnyard dog that barks at cats and bays at the moon. We are at present also babysitting the cat of my wife's sister. The two animals have become chummy; a Maine word you might not know, just think friendly. Not so the dog of my boyhood. Rover was a dog's dog. He loved to chase chickens and cats, and when he could get away with it, cows and cars. He barked at anything that moved, except in the house where he was only allowed on cold nights and special occasions. His sound was refreshing, not irritating to me. He was the one stabilizing creature in a farmyard of constant activity. He taught me how to slow down and take it easy by his barks and barking and baying!

There was always a 'to do' list on the Blackstone Homestead. Buildings to be painted, rocks to be picked, barrels to be prepared for harvest, bins to be swept, and chicken coups to be cleaned. Rover's bark was a call to an unhurried lifestyle, living, and life. His **'bow wow'** was a warning that life taken to serious can bring on serious problems, and as my county cousin Clayton (also a pastor like me of 44 years) once wrote, "it is high time we take a lesson from man's best friend and listen to what he is telling us by his barking beatitudes":

1. Never pass up the opportunity to go for a joy ride.

BARKING

2. Allow the experience of fresh air and the wind in your face to be pure ecstasy.
3. When loved ones come home, always run to greet them.
4. When it's in your best interest, practice obedience.
5. Let others know when they have invaded your territory.
6. Take naps and stretch before rising.
7. Run, romp, and play daily.
8. Eat with gusto and enthusiasm.
9. Be loyal.
10. Never pretend to be something you're not.
11. If what you want lies buried, dig until you find it.
12. When someone is having a bad day, be silent, sit close by, and nuzzle them gently.
13. Thrive on attention and let people touch you.
14. Avoid biting when a simple growl will do.
15. On hot days, drink lots of water and lie under a shade tree.
16. When you're happy, dance around and wag your entire body.
17. Delight in the simple joy of a long walk.
18. No matter how often you're scolded, don't buy into the guilt thing and pout. Run right back and make friends.
19. Show yourself friendly and just maybe you might find a 'best-friend'!

Funny, what a dog's bark can teach humans about living! Isn't this what we have been trying to understand from the important Biblical verses that helped us start remembering the actions and antics of a boyhood friend, a 'best-friend', a dog named Rover: **"But ask now the beasts, and they shall teach thee . . . who knoweth not in all these that the hand of the Lord hath wrought this."** (Job 12:7, 9)

FENCE

Spring was not only planting season on my childhood homestead in Perham, Maine, but fence building season as well. We had to go around the miles (and I mean miles) of fence line and see what posts had to be replaces as we reconnected the wire to those posts after the winter had passed. Then it was time we put the dairy cows out to pasture after the long Maine winter had kept them cooped up in the stales of the cow barn. I have a lot of memories of those fence lines and a dog named Rover in the back corner of my homestead memory.

A two-strand, high-tensile electric fence, with the top strand being electrified, worked well when trying to keep a Holstein herd in check throughout the summer months on the farm. A sound electric fence with a sufficient charge would deter most cows from venturing outside the pasture boundary. I still see the small box setting on a shelf located on the staircase which took you to the basement of our barn. (It was a short in that line that would eventually burn-down my boyhood barn!) The electronics of that box would send a pulse of high voltage along the wire creating an open circuit. A cow touching the fence would complete the circuit, allowing the current to go through the cow's body to the ground giving the animal a shock, and hopefully enough deterrent to keep them behind the wire? Of course, cows weren't the only ones that got a shock; a dog's best friend did too, but why?

I remember one of the rites of manhood on the homestead was mustering enough courage to grab hold of the electric fence. If the ground under your feet was dry, the jolt was tolerable and even manageable. I learned very early that you had to pick your spots to impress your younger cousins. It was more psychological than painful. With a fence line running for miles, the juice on the line wasn't always that strong. More often than not, the cow was keep in by the remembrance of a bad experience, like touching the wire while standing in a puddle of water, so too with a cousin. Baiting a cousin went something like this. I would demonstrate my courage by holding onto the fence in an area where I knew there were a shortage, and the grass dry. Terrified, my younger cousins would stand amazed. Asking them if they would like to try, more often than not they would refuse. However, in time, the temptation would become too great for them. On another day and time, usually after a nice shower, I would ask again. Having already proven myself I would not have to touch the hot wire again, but tempting and teasing I would convince them that to really be a man you had to grab hold. Even Rover barked with laughter! Sometimes I see now just how cruel I was to my younger cousins. It took me awhile in my boyhood to learn Jesus classic precept: **"Therefore all things whatsoever ye would that man should do to you, do ye even so to them: for this is the law and the prophets."** (Matthew 7:12)

I remember spending days maintaining the fence line. As the summer lengthened the grass would grow up around the fence and start shorting it out. With a hand scythe, Rover and I would make our rounds around the fence. Often a cow would rub up against a post and break it, or a moose would walk through it. Fence repair was priority one when a call came that the herd was out. A fence check soon located the trouble and a repair had to be done. I enjoyed building a new fence with Gramp. Cedar poles, wire wrapped around old barrels, ceramic insulators, crowbars, a pail full of clips and nails, one dog, and a big sledge hammer in the rock cart meant that a new fence had to be built somewhere on the homestead. Gramp liked his fence straight and solid, as he did his grandsons. It is still amazing to me what those few tiny wires would keep in, keep out, and keep up!

SLED

MANY YEARS AGO I went to pick up my daughter from an afternoon of sliding with her youth group at the White Birches in Hancock, Maine. The White Birches is a golf course set on the side of a steep hill which in the winter time turns into a marvelous place to slide. The owner (Crazy Gill) allowed the children from the area to use it as their own personal sliding arena. As I neared the spot, my mind transgressed to a place where I too had a wonderful time sliding with my family cousins, neighborhood friends, and a dog named Rover.

How times have changed! Plastic sleds and saucers are now the norm. Sheets of hard plastic of all shapes could be seen gliding down the hill at the White Birches. Oh, there was the occasional toboggan, and a few intertubes were in sight, but something was missing? Snowmobiles could be seen pulling the kids back up the hill after their long rides almost to the small pond that was located at the end of the main fairway. A four-wheeler could also be seen carting the children back up the hill, but something was still missing? As I pondered this peaceful scene on that wintry day it hit me like a thunder bolt! What are missing were my old wooden sled and my boyhood friend Rover.

What a beauty she was (sled); what a beauty he was (Rover)! Thin iron tracks ran on both side braced every few feet to the frame. Wooden slats ran her entire length, all five feet of her. There were small spaces between each slat which made her light and streamlined. Up front were the two handles for steering, also made of wood. She was both maneuverable and manageable, unlike the sleds of today. Granted, in deep snow she was useless, but on crust and ice she was like 'grease lightening', and there was even room for that beautiful dog. A long length of rope was attached to the

SLED

handle bars for pulling, no four-wheelers or snowmobiles in those days to pull us back up the hill. Arm strong power and a bit of help from Rover's powerful jaws and neck was the only power we needed to get us back up the slope for another run.

As my mind went back in time I could see myself and Rover at the starting mark, ready to descend the Blackstone Homestead sliding course. The driveway at my father's old house is U-shaped. In the winter Dad would cut the U at its base with a bank of snow creating a backward S around the farmhouse and the barn. After a slight warm up and a quick freeze Dad's driveway became the best sliding track in the world. If the amount of snow was deep, the old Farmall tractor would have plowed up huge banks of snow all along the track exposing the driveway to a buildup of hard snow and slippery ice. The conditions were ideal for a recorded breaking run. To gain the initial momentum, I would pick up my sled and start at the entrance of the two door garage across the road. When I reached the top of the driveway I would place the sled on the ice and jump aboard. Grabbing the handle bars I would settle on the sled, but within moments I would have to pull hard to the right. Going straight ahead I would crash into the massive cow barn. Immediately, thereafter I would have to pull hard left lest I run into the snow bank near the house; where upon I had a straight run into the pasture below. What run! I can still feel the wind in my face. More often than not Rover would run alongside and we would meet at the bottom of the run and walk together back to the top of the driveway for another run, and if I could convince him we would slide double! What days a boy can have with his dog when God " **. . . casteth for His ice like morsels: who can stand before His cold?**" (Psalms 147:17) The answer is simple: a lad and his dog and a snow sled!

MORNING

As I ABSENTMINDEDLY SET down at my desk to begin another day pastoring the people of Emmanuel Baptist Church of Ellsworth, Maine, I watch the final falling flakes of a night snowstorm through my study window. It is but a lovely afterthought of a wintry night that has just past, but a marvelous memory of a day long since gone when I was much younger. It is on mornings like this that my mind seems to drift back to a childhood morning on the Blackstone Homestead in Perham, Maine and to a boyhood friend that was always awake to greet me every morning.

It is the early 1960's, and I am a child again, and the newly fallen snow has turned our farm into a winter wonderland. Another day has begun on the family farm that sets in a beautiful dale between two Aroostook County hills. As I make my way through the pantry I am greeted by my dog Rover. His wagging tail tells me he is happy to see me up. Our conversation together passes the time it takes for me to dress and to make my way across the yard to the huge cow barn now covered with three inches of fresh fallen snow. The frosty air makes everything smell clean, and my frosty breath only adds to the mystery of the morning as Rover and I head for our morning responsibilities in the barn. I notice cat tracks between the house and the barn, to which I reply, "The cats are up, Rover; won't you have fun this morning." The morning is peaceful and quiet. The silence is only broken by the mooing of a Holstein wanting her breakfast, and the cackling of a hen awaiting her oats. All along the way an occasional bark it heard as Rover clears his throat. These sounds are heard as I open the door to the barn.

As I make my way into the barn, the only light to be seen is from the door at the far end of the barn leading to the cows

MORNING

below. As I pass the old truck which always was parked there in the winter, I pick up my basketball from off the truck body. Shooting at the backboard hanging on one of the middle rafter, frost flies everywhere as the ball swishes through the net. "I still have it," I spoke to Rover as he barks in approval of the made shot. Then I stop to feed the hens. The ninety and nine greet me at the door, as I throw grain around the floor of the chicken coup. As the chickens gather in their breakfast I see how many eggs are in the nests. Rover waits patiently at the door as I finish the collection. "Mum will be pleased," I told Rover, "Twenty-seven in all."

Making my way down the stair into the cellar, I hear my Father humming an old hymn of the faith, as he spent a little time with his God. Dad is the only man I ever knew that could take care of cows and worship God at the same time. The warm stalls felt good against the cold upstairs, as I made my way in front of the young cows to feed them. Rover has parked himself on the steps knowing he wasn't allowed any further into the basement of the cow barn. Dad had the cows almost cleaned out as he turned with a smile and a wink hearing my voice talking with Rover. Dad never said much, but I knew he was always pleased when I came to the barn to help him with the chores.

After our tasks were finished we make our way back to the old farm house were Mother always had a big breakfast waiting. A Blackstone Homestead morning was nicely underway, and another day with my best friend as well! In my early Biblical training I noticed this was exactly how God began his days: " **. . . and the morning were the first day . . . and the morning were the second day . . . and the morning were the third day . . . and the morning were the fourth day . . . and the morning were the fifth day . . . and the morning were the sixth day . . .** " (Genesis 1:5, 8, 13, 19, 23, 31) Mornings and dogs go together! (Footnote: this was the very first Blackstone Homestead Memory I ever wrote. After its writing on November 1, 1988, I thought I would never write another story, but at this compiling I have written nearly a thousand. It is just interesting to me that Rover shows up in my first recorded boyhood memory!)

DOG

I READ IN A book once this classic statement: *"The more I see of people, the better I like dogs!"* The older I get I understand this cynic's point of view, and surely by now you have recognized that I thought more of my boyhood friend, Rover, than I did people!

Rover grew up with me on our family farm in Perham, Maine. Rover was German, but had no aristocratic ancestors, and he was Collie, but won no blue ribbons at the local dog shows. Rover was just a dog, a plain, old, ordinary dog, but he was my friend and that was good enough for me. I don't ever remember needing protection as a child, but I am confident in writing now that if the situation or circumstance would have happened that I needed a bodyguard Rover would have been at my side in a flash.

Our best times were roaming and wandering times when we went for a walk in the paths through the woods that surrounded our farmhouse. As I think back, I wonder if I was ever more happy in my boyhood than when Rover and I would head out on a warming May morning from our homestead with the trees blooming and the grass exploding along the lanes between my father's side of the farm and my grandfather's side of the homestead; a distance of about a mile as the crow flies, the way Rover and I always like to go. It was a time when the bees were out working the blossoms, the mosquitos were looking for blood, and the cows were enjoying the first taste of sweet grass after a long, Maine winter on dry, bland hay. It was a time for a boy and his dog to ramble and rumble!

I never knew a morning when Rover wasn't as keen as I was for a wilderness walk. I have since those days wondered what Rover was wondering about as we strolled along. I know he wondered why I never chased the woodland creatures like he liked to do. I knew he had a deep, profound philosophy of **"a bird, a cat in**

the mouth was worth two in the bush!" I never saw Rover catch anything in his life, but that didn't stop him from trying, even on our walks, our wanderings, our strolls and ramblings to Grandfather's house! After a few trips I came to conclusion it was the treats we got from grandmother that motivated his journeys with me. I thought more often than not he just like being with me, but he also liked the rewards he got when he got home as well.

The lesson that has come to me through these childhood experience with a dog is the fact that a country boy with a Rover can have more fun in a May morning walk through the woods than a vacationer can have in Vegas in a month. That a boy and his dog can find more pleasure in a romp through the trees than all the vacationists have on a Caribbean cruise. That a lad and his animal, best friend can find more joy in a forenoon than a two-week vacation in Paris (I have been to Paris, I spent an afternoon in Paris in 2001, and I have never had a desire to return, I had had my fill!).

To this day I can reconstruct in my mind some of the trails Rover and I use to take: the path through the apple orchard behind Gramp's house; the lane behind the massive cow barn that would often get Rover's woolly mane full of burdocks; the trail down by the brook that often got both of us wet before we headed for home, and the track, yes, a railroad track below our house that took us deep into the woods. The heart of Africa was no more remote than these passageways through the Blackstone woodland. Occasionally Rover and I would stare wistfully into a region we never explored, but discretion prevailed and we contented ourselves with how far we had come and wisely turned around and head for home. Wise is the boy and dog who knows the proper time to: " **. . . turn back . . .** " (Jeremiah 49:8)

LANE

HAVING JUST RETURNED FROM a walk up town, I once again am at my laptop computer with a memory to share about my boyhood, best friend Rover. As I wound my way through the streets and avenues and boulevards of Ellsworth, from the post office to the bank, I recalled less hectic days when I traveled from point A to point B; a day when you didn't have to fight the traffic of a turnpike and the payment of a toll road. I guess my recent 1700 mile trip to visit my brother in Pennsylvania is also on my mind. So as I started and stopped at every intersection watching right and left for oncoming cars, I remembered the times I use to walk the lanes in my hometown with my dog Rover.

If you remember a lane your probably like me over sixty and lived on a farm. Younger people today don't even know what a lane is, despite it being the main connection between villages and towns and cities for the better part of the last century. We use to call them a dirt road, but now that progress has come even to Perham, Maine they have been covered over with asphalt so we can speed from point A to point B faster. If a dirt road is the common name for these country streets, then "county lane" must be the formal title.

My mind's eye still can see the lane that connected the main building of our homestead with the Paul Place, a collection of fields on the back side of the farm, a favorite strolling lane for me and Rover. This two track road worked its way up through the dale which separated two huge fields located directly behind the main cow barn. The lane was not a mile long, but miles and miles of memories now floods through my mind as I ponder the times I spend on and around that lane with my furry friend.

How many hundreds of loads of hay did I ride through that lane from clover field to hayloft as Rover barked? How many

LANE

tractor rides did I experience over that bumpy lane going or coming with plow, harrow, or rack as Rover walked beside me? How many walks did I take through that lane to hunt partridge, rabbit, and woodchuck in the fields and forest surrounding that lane with my hunting companion? If I could return to that grassy avenue today each foot of its length would generate a memory of passed days with Rover and my cousins, or other family members. I can see Uncle Reed on the back of the manure sled as we took that lane to the back pasture to spread manure in the month of February, but no Rover then, remember Rover hated winter. I can see Dad bouncing up and down on the old John Deer tractor pulling the sprayer as he makes his way over that lane to the frog pond for water; Rover never liked spraying either! I can see my cousin Dale learning how to drive the old green International pickup truck on that lane as Clayton and I went along as instructors and Rover went along for the ride. I can see Gramp Carroll walking through that lane that at certain times of the year doubled as a cow path, as he and his dog (Gramp also loved Rover) rounded up the herd for afternoon milking. I can see Uncle Clayton driving the Ford truck loaded with potato barrels as we moved from the Russell Place to the Paul Place during digging and Rover loved when we dug the potatoes because of the kids that came onto the homestead to help with the harvest, and I can still see Rover returning from an afternoon hunt up that lane.

Obviously, a mental walk down a quiet Blackstone lane is a walk down memory lane as well. In one of Jesus' famous parables, He speaks of going into the " **. . . streets and lanes of a city . . .** " (Luke 14:21) as I did today. As I pondered my return from those streets and lanes of coastal Ellsworth and remembered a lane from my boyhood I think I like the country lane best because on the lanes of Ellsworth I found no Rover today!

STREAM

PERHAM IS A SMALL farming community tucked neatly in the foothills of Northern Maine. The rolling hills in central Aroostook County create small valleys were feeder streams cascade their way to the primary watershed of the area, the Aroostook River. The stream that runs through Perham is called Salmon Stream. Its source is a ten acre lake which fills one of those Aroostook County valleys just about three miles from my father's house. From a knoll just south of that lake you can not only see the stream that comes out of the lake meandering all the way to Washburn and the Aroostook, but part of my father's 720 acre farm as well. Rover and I loved to walk along 'her' banks, fish in 'her' belly, and sit by 'her' brooks; and other small stream that feed 'her'. One of those brooks started just behind my homestead house, and worked its way through field and forest until they met. Rover and I loved those brooks and stream and creeks that feed the Salmon; just as the Psalmist writes: **"He brought streams also out of the rock, and caused waters to run down like rivers."** (Psalm 78:16)!

I find it interesting how nature imitates life. We meet thousands of people in our lifetime, but why is it we make friends of only a few; just like dogs. It is the same with the places we go. I have been to Australia, India, France, Israel, and England and back; I have lived in three states, and have travelled the length of Canada from Alaska. I have seen hundreds of places, but only a very few bring a smile to my face when after a long absence I return. I still smile every time I cross "her" heading for the homestead. (I crossed 'her' just a few days again to bury my father and son side by side in the family plot in FairView Cemetery. As I crossed 'her' I recalled the first day I ever took my son Scott fishing. He was two and a half and we were living in the Dow house just around the corner. Scott threw his first worm into a small pool just below the culvert. We didn't catch anything that day, but our fishing adventures had begun and we would have plenty of them before his unexpected death. I told my daughter of this memory as we travelled over the brook the next morning to plant flowers by Scott's grave. As we dug the first hole a small angleworm came crawling out!) Salmon Stream was a place were old friends lived, or at least once lived. Each time I'm home I wonder if my old friend's relatives still live there. Perhaps the offspring of that giant trout Dad caught in "her" Dead Water Hole when I was just a boy and Rover was just a pup are around. The very first trout I ever caught on a fly came out of Salmon Brook, I often wondered if its relations like flies, and what of Rover?

Becoming close to a brook or creek as I was to this stream is like the companionship of a dog. First you must be introduced. You must get acquainted through dates. Fishermen call them "trips". Second you must be instructed. Like dogs, each stream is different. Each holds their own mystic and magic. Each has to be handled just right. Lastly you must be inspired. What was it about Rover when I first meet him? I had met many other farm dogs, and had even liked some, but Rover was different; I loved him. Salmon Stream is different because she flows through part of my beloved homestead, and she holds Dad's favorite fishing hole; a pool he fished in until he was 92. (Dad passed away into heaven before the fishing season of his 94th year, in the same winter as my son!) Often you hear fishermen speak of a body of water in the feminine gender, as I have done. "What a beautiful lake "she" is!" "Isn't "she" a pretty pond?" But I have come to believe that in order to develop a lasting relationship it takes a long friendship, a love affair if you will.

When I was young I was introduced to "her", and I was instructed about "her", and in time I was inspired by "her". As I write this article you can see that I am still moved by the thought of "her". A year ago before my father's death I returned to my family's farm and once again my Dad and I walked "her" banks, and cast our flies into "her" bowels. The beavers had dammed "her" just

STREAM

below "her" dead water hole, but she was still alive as "her" water from" her" countless creeks continued to flow through the heart of the homestead. The only thing that was missing was my dear dog Rover! It was Job that wrote of this aspect of a dog and a stream: "**. . . and as the stream of brooks they pass away.**" (Job 6:15) The water that once flowed through Salmon Stream is gone, just like my best friend in my boyhood!

URGE

I HAVE ALWAYS HAD the urge to record my past. Contained within the filing cabinets of my church study are boxes filled with keepsakes, memorabilia, and notebooks of my life. It is an urge some of us have more than others, this need to record our legacy. An urge to prepare for the day when the mind needs nourishment that can only come from "the stores of the soul"; as is the case in my attempting to remember a childhood friend of the animal kingdom. Paul spoke to Timothy about "**. . . laying up in store for themselves a good foundation against the time to come . . .** " (I Timothy 6:19) This is what I am trying to do in the compiling of this series of remembrances about my boyhood, best-friend Rover and my homestead history!

    I have always been fascinated with those who stayed to face the blight and bleakness of a Maine winter. Hearty souls who prepared well, and were willing to endure anything thrown at them, or in a Maine winter, dumped on them! The squirrel and the chickadee come to mind immediately, as does the Blackstones. I never remember my parents or grandparents heading for Florida to wait out winter. The garden had been canned, and the orchard put in barrels. The fatted cow and pig had been stored away in the freezer, and the spuds safely deposited in the underground, potato storage. With their stores in they knew they could survive snow season, no matter how deep the snow or cold the air. Perhaps this is why I write. I know there is a dark day approaching in my life and the lives of my homestead family. A day when there will be no more crops, no more cousins, and no more cows on the homestead. (That day came in the 1990s when after 130 years the farm was put to rest. It was only restored in 2016 when two Amish families from Pennsylvania bought the farm and returned it to its dairy days!)

URGE

A time when life as we once knew it will be gone. What will we do then? Move away from our heritage, and forget that time ever happened? I think not! It is for this reason I have complied these memories of my boyhood dog named Rover. It is my way of storing up that which my early life produced and my link to a time in my life when I was at peace and all things were right with the world because I had a constant friend and companion in a dog.

Flipping through this storehouse of recollections, I witness again the hallelujah sounds of my past; the spectacular sights that still shine brightly in the yesterdays of my boyhood memory. I witness again that first fish as it strikes my "chicken coup" worm with Rover's encouragement coming from the 'amen corner' . . . I smell again the appealing aroma of a field of clover just cut as does Rover's nose . . . I hear again the bark of my favorite dog Rover as he greets me as I step off the school bus . . . I experience again the thrill of driving a tractor for the first time with Rover on the seat . . . I watch again as the crow fight's off a flight of sparrows; when Rover wished he could fly . . . I enjoy again the sight of my first robin in spring that Rover chases . . . I admire again a full harvest moon reflected off a potato field just put in stores and the shadow of Rover . . . I laugh again as my cousin gets a shock off the electric fence surrounding the pasture and Rover seems to get a kick out of it as well . . . I roll again in a lawn filled with dandelions in a wrestling match with Rover. (My first attempt in recording these memories was in a book I called "Homestead Homilies" published by Resource Publication from Wipf and Stock Publishers in 2017.)

For those of us who choose to stay in the abandoned places of society (like many parts of Maine are) these memories will help us endure the harsh season before us. These stores of memories and remembrances will nourish us until the spring comes and we get the urge to once again return to the sacred sod of our birth, dog or no dog!

DAWNING

IT WAS THE OLD saga Job who lamented, "When I lie down, I say, when shall I arise and the night is gone? And I am full of tossings to and fro until the dawning of the day." (Job 7:4) I will be the first to admit that mornings are not my best times, but I remember someone who loved the dawning of the day more than any other part of the day! For my boyhood, best friend Rover, the forenoon (my grandfather's word for morning) was the time we started our day together, and for him that was as good as it got.

In this age of fast, faster, and fastest there is still one thing man has not been able to hurry: the dawning of a new day, nor the companionship of a boy and his dog. Some wish they could, and other, like city dwellers, try by their artificial lights to keep it daytime throughout the nighttime, but no matter, for it will dawn only when God's eternal clock says it's time to start a new day. It was my dog Rover that reminded me every morning just what a precious gift a dawning day was.

When you lived on a working potato and dairy farm you had ample opportunities to witness the glorious splendor of the birth of a morning. Few today take the time to watch darkness turn into day. Most would say, "I've seen that before." Whether through the old milking shed door carrying milk to the large milk cans on the old International pickup, or riding a tractor on the back forty doing some early morning field work, the early light from the eastern sky was awe inspiring to me because of Rover. You might ask how could I tell: was it the wagging tail or the joyful barking at the sun? And as God takes time beginning each and every new day, I learned from a barnyard dog so should I!

It still takes time for me to wake up after I get up. Even my wife has learned not to communicate with me before noon, for like

DAWNING

the dawn I slowly come into the world. Despite the season, or setting our clocks ahead in the spring and behind in the fall, nothing has ever changed natures wake up call. We can rush through it; we can try to hurry it; we can speed up our lives with instant this and instant that, but no matter, for the dawn will keep to its deliberate, delicate, and determined timetable no matter what we do, and even my boyhood dog demonstrated to me the importance of cherishing the heavenly dawning of a new day, a new day for adventure, a new day to just be together and alive.

This attempt by man to hurry the dawn is only a sign of a deeper problem facing him. It is the root transgression of discontentment. We hurry through breakfast thinking lunch will be better. I don't even waste my time to eat in the morning; I'd rather feast on the dawning of the day with a dog, or as the case is today a cat called Eddie. We hurry through marriages thinking the next one will certainly be greater. My wife and I just celebrated forty-four years, and we are still in the wonderful dawning of our relationship. We hurry up our children's childhood only to make them as the devotional writer Vance Havner put it, **"Precocious kids-all vine and no roots."** We tear open the cocoon to soon in so many areas of our lives only to reveal a dead butterfly, beautiful, but dead.

Mornings, and marriages, and Marnie's (That's my daughter's name) take time to unfold and develop, and only we have the control to let them mature at God's pace. Could I suggest a dog can help in this vital area? It was my dog that helped me put into proper perspective the dawning of a new day. Animals seem to have that ability to slow down time, helping us to take time with life, and put time in its proper place.

Ever since that early lesson from my boyhood, best friend, I have tried to let life progress at its own rate, not mine. It has made for some spectacular sunrises in my life.

FLASHBACK

Spring in northern Maine is a special season, a resurrection time, a flashback to a time in the changing of a young man's life. It is a time to break away from the long confinement of a cold winter and *"roam at random."* To go; to just go and see what is about in the fields and forests of the homestead with your dog Rover.

It happened years ago in the yestermorn of my past, while still living on my father's farm in Perham, Maine. Rover and I were restless that morning, as we often were. We left the farm house early with no particular destination in mind. We walked up the country lane that passed our home until we reached our neighbor's house (the McDougal's). Turning left, we headed into the woods by way of a rough road that lead to a series of small fields surrounded by forestland. In a matter of a few minutes we spotted a group of squirrels watching us intently from their lofty lookouts high up in a cluster of maple trees. Their morning chatter stopped as they checked out these intruders from the open-country. They watched us carefully as we tried to get as close to them as we could. One fatal bark by Rover sent them scurrying higher into the trees as our stalking came to an end; much too soon for me, but just right for Rover, who wanted to move on.

It was a cool morning as I remember it. Broken clouds drifted across the sun, as we walked deeper into the woods. The mossy floor of the forest felt good under our feet. A light breeze blowing through the leaves of the trees made a soothing sound in our ears. Our eyes were focused ahead as a rabbit, half white and half brown, jumped from behind a bush and soon disappeared in the undergrowth. Little did he know we weren't hunting him on this day? Thinking of that rabbit as I wandered, his condition was characteristic of spring; anticipating the covering of summer, but still exhibiting the markings of winter; kind of how I felt that morning as I was fighting, struggling with the reality of growing up; that middle ground between boyhood and adolescence.

Eventually we left the woods for an open field located along the Salmon Lake Road. As we stepped out from cover, a flock of crows feeding under and old apple tree took flight. Their noisy ascent told of their displeasure at our interrupting their breakfast. Walking over to see what they had been feeding on we soon discovered the remains of another rabbit, a cousin to the one we jumped just a few minutes before probably? No doubt killed by a bobcat or a fox, the leftovers were but a few bones and a little fur. Caught in the transformation of seasons, the bunny had become vulnerable because of his two-tone color; how I was feeling that morning, neither boy nor man. I knew Rover had settled the issue long before, for Rover was well into old-age on that early spring stroll through the backyard of my youth!

Crossing the hay end of the field, we swung towards home. Turning the corner by the road, a pair of partridges ran before us. Stopping, so they might stop, we watched as these birds, fleet of foot, out-ran our vision. As if transfixed, we stared at them long after they had gone out of sight. Their cries are still echoing in my ears to this day. Their plumage is still visible in my eyes to this morning. Their memory is still remembered in my mind as you can see. They were a fabulous finale to a farmland flashback with a favorite friend.

Spring scrambles and rural rambles are a wonderful way to spend a morning, whether in reality, or remembrance. The ability to flashback is in the memory, a wonderful and marvellous gift the Creator gave to His creature called man. It was Solomon that wrote: **"The memory of the just is blessed . . . "** (Proverbs 10:7) Aren't flashbacks fun?

BLIZZARD

THE SNOW WAS COMING down fast, and the wind was blowing the fluffy mixture around with a fury. I knew that within a very short time our homestead house would be isolated from the rest of the homes in north Perham. A severe, mid-winter blizzard had hit suddenly, unexpectedly, but we were ready as we always were, and so was my dog Rover; he knew just where he wanted to be and needed to be.

I remember Dad coming in shortly before five, saying, "It's a wild one out there!" He had left the main homestead barn where he had been helping my grandfather Carroll and Uncle Read and Uncle Clayton milk the Holstein herd. "Gramp said I ought to get home before the road became impassible," my father continued, as Rover settled into his corner by the pantry door. I watched as he licked the icy clumps of snow off his paws and the icicles off his fur. Rover had just come in from a few minutes of play in the snow with his best friend; for we believed in Job's philosophy: **"Hast thou entered into the treasures of the snow?"** (Job 38:22). We loved running and jumping in the white stuff, wading in the deep stuff, and our favorite, building snow tunnels in the huge snow banks that surrounded the barnyard from sometimes late November to sometimes early April, or at least back in Rover's days! Rover always seems to know when a big storm was upon us. His actions imitated a Maine black bear getting ready to go into hibernation.

The next words out of Dad's mouth were, "Barry, let's get to the barn and finish the chores before supper." Across the barnyard from our home was another huge cow barn. Down cellar in that barn were the young cattle. Just above them was a chicken coup, and behind the wall in front of the cows was a small potato storage area. Quickly putting on my heavy winter coat and boots, I

BLIZZARD

followed Dad out through the pantry and down the stairs and through the woodshed to the blizzard outside. As I walked out the shed door I knew it must be bad outside, Rover wasn't following; he was staying inside. If I hadn't known the barn was there, I would have asked Dad where he was leading me. I cover my face with my scarf and headed across the yard. The wind was so strong and the snow so heavy that three foot drifts had already been created between the house and the barn. There was even a few times in my short trip across the yard that I lost sight of Dad. I thought to myself, "What a blizzard; the worst of the season!"

By the time Dad got to the small door that opened to the interior of the cow barn, I had caught up with him. As we kicked the snow away from the entrance, I took the piece of wood out of the latch that held the door closed. Once inside I placed a bale of hay against the door, so the snow wouldn't drift onto the floor. Covering the floor was a layer of sawdust and a layer of straw, a very good isolation for both the cows and the potatoes below. I immediately headed for the chicken coup as Dad when downstairs to start cleaning out the young cows. After gathering the eggs and filling both the feed bens and water bowls, I went downstairs to help Dad finish up. Giving each cow and calf a measure of grain and some hay finished the process. I noticed that Dad didn't even take the manure outside that night; he would leave it for the morning chores, when the blizzard had blown itself out, and had died down a bit!

Retracing our steps, we returned to the house wet and white. Stopping off at the wood pile, both Dad and I carried an arm load of wood to the wood box in the pantry. Rover was waiting for us when we entered the kitchen, dry and warm! He had chosen well to stay inside with a fierce, 'nor'easter' blowing a gale outside!

CREEK

The Blackstone Homestead history is a long history (1861-2017); full of colorful critters and terrain tales. Documented in only a few shattered letters and diaries, this history, at least for me, is worthy to be recorded for those of Blackstone roots who will never get a chance to know what it was like to live on that beautiful land and with friendly animals, like a dog named Rover!

The concept of beauty (**"Beautiful for situation, the joy of the whole earth . . . "**—Psalm 48:2) is of course totally in the eye of the beholder. I have seen beauty in a can of worms dug from the fenced in area around the chicken coup and the beautiful brook trout they have caught. I have called beautiful what others would call ugly. A fresh spread field of mature sounds smelly and unattractive, but to a boy with six generations of Blackstone blood flowing through his veins there is beauty there as well. (Believe it or not, one of the reasons I believed I found my life's mate was the day my wife Coleen chose to ride with me while I spread mature across a field below my childhood home!) A newborn Holstein is a beautiful sight, as is a field of Katahdin potatoes in full bloom. I lived with beauty four seasons of the year; beauty unmatched by any place I have ever lived since. The shores and shoals of the coast of Maine cannot be compared to the hills and hollows of the homestead. The heat and humidity of Kerala (India) cannot be matched by the cool and cold of the farm. The 'green pastures' and 'still waters' (Psalm 23:2) of Israel can't be compared to the green pastures and still waters of Perham. The pragmatists, realists, and modernists will no doubt say my memories are nothing but sentimentality, so be it! I write not for them, but for me and those who will one day wish they still owned a piece of the Blackstone farm (as I do but piece by piece it is being purchased by Amish families

CREEK

from Pennsylvania). I need to be reminded in this very ugly world, just what a beautiful dog I had, a beautiful life I had, and **" . . . the perfection of beauty . . . "** (Psalm 50:2). For those of us who live or love the country, we make no apology, no excuses for our behavior and language for *"all things bright and beautiful!"*

One of my favorite and most beautiful memories involves the image of a young boy walking the banks of a creek with his dog in springtime. I see them basking in the warmth of the first truly spring day of the year as they chase a homemade boat down the creek bed by their homestead house. The creek had widened its banks because of the melting snow in the forest just beyond the lane that passed their homestead home. Never wider than six feet, the creek flowed clear through the culvert where he launched his battleship. Its course hugged a hay field until it reached the huge cow barn of their barnyard. From there the pitch of the land dramatically increases as did the speed of his dreadnought heading for battle. The boy's dog, Rover, splashes in and out of the current nipping at the boat, as the boy weighs the temptation between getting wet and getting yelled at by his mum for getting wet? The verdict is to get wet as his warship got caught on an icy shoal!

The boy and his best friend continue their mission along the bank of the creek to the pasture behind the barn. Snow banks were still obstacles to their progress, but nothing seems too able to stop their quest to reach the spot were the creek reentered the woods below the pasture. It was there in a small pond the battle against their imaginary enemy would take place, and the war would be won or lost in that isolated and beautiful spot!

It is unimaginably sad to think that there is a generation of young people growing up in this land without the imagination to play along a brook; let alone so shortsighted to see beauty in a small creek with a dog! I have come to the conclusion that I must be content with the theology of Solomon when he wrote: **" . . . He hath made everything beautiful in his time . . . to everything there is a season and a time to every purpose . . . "** (Ecclesiastes 3:11, 1)

THURSDAY

NESTLED AT THE BASE of a rolling hill, in a cedar swamp near the farm's equipment graveyard, was an area we called the Paul Place (named after the family that uses to own the fields and forest): a place Rover and I loved to walk and think.

Back in the 1960's, my father would take me to this part of the farm to help plant potatoes, or sow oats, depending on the year of rotation. We use to hunt partridge in an apple orchard located in a fenced off section for the young Holstein cows. It was in a hay field not far from the swamp I shot my first ground hog and later in my teens my first bear (I was a hunter then, but preferred as I grew older to fishing rather than hunting; was part of the reason for the dramatic change, the passing of my hunting dog Rover?). For years, this old farm served as an additional source of land for the homestead. The ground was rocky and hilly, yet it produced year after year. I believe it became Rover's favorite place on the Blackstone Homestead to wander and wonder, romp and ramble!

Throughout my boyhood and into my teens, the Paul Place was a working place. I spent many a Thursday of my childhood hoeing and picking rocks in that place. My earliest memory of the Paul Place was the Thursday I drove truck for the first time during potato harvest. I could hardly stay in the seat because of the slope of the hill and my short legs. Hanging onto the steering wheel tightly, I did manage to bounce my way down through the field. I recall the Thursday Dad sent me out to rake the hay. That year the Paul Place was a field of clover. One of my favorite jobs on the farm was preparing a hay field for baling. It was a hot morning in July as I mounted the old Farmall tractor after hitching up the ancient circular rake. It was a slow ride from the tool shed on the main farm to the Paul Place over the winding field road that connected

THURSDAY

them, but the air was fresh and the sky was clear, a perfect day for haying, and to top it off Rover was there.

I also remember the Thursday Rover and me walking to the Paul Place to pick raspberries. Along the tree line, just above the cedar swamp, grew a line of raspberry bushes unequalled except for a patch on the Salmon Lake Road near my homestead house. Standing as high as I was tall, the raspberry bushes yield exceptional berries, good for pies, jams, and tarts, but not for Rover; he only liked one Barry.

These Thursdays on the Paul Place were also times I dreamed of the future and where I would travel (I must admit I never dreamed of Australia, India, England, Canada, France, or Israel). In my younger years, I often pictured myself as a soldier fighting on a far-off battlefield in Vietnam. I imagined myself as accomplishing great things, but never thinking I had already discovered one of my life's best places with life's best friend. I took the Paul Place and Rover for granted on those Thursdays of my youth, and now on this Thursday in the year 2017 the Paul Place will soon be sold to an Amish family? For the first time since 1861, the farm is being sold off one section at a time. My brother (the last owner of the homestead) finished farming in the 1990's and returned to school to become a history teacher, and as a second occupation, a police officer. How long will it be before the farm road that leads to the Paul Place fades from my memory? How long before the field on the side hill will belong to somebody else? How long before the cedar swamp is cut over? How long before a Thursday in my future comes and the Paul Place will simply go away as Rover did?

The Psalmist once wrote: **"So teach us to number our days, that we may apply our hearts unto wisdom."** (Psalm 90:12) Those days included my Thursdays on the Paul Place, so what did I learn: that days and dogs pass away, but not in your memory or that is my hope, and if it does, God forbid, I hope somebody will read to me these memories and I can in that moment remember again!

CHILDHOOD

INTO THE AROOSTOOK COUNTY of Maine in 1951 Barry Alan Blackstone was born. The Korean War was raging in the Far East with General MacArthur's forces pushing the North Koreans and Chinese back to the 38th parallel. By mid-March, just a few days after Barry's birth, a much-battered Seoul, Korea was recaptured by a United Nation's Army, but this suffering and hardship did not touch Barry in his Northern Maine refuge. Barry's was a quiet and peaceful childhood, one of delight and discovery, void of struggle for survival! And there to make Barry's life even more pleasant was a dog named Rover!

In his earliest years, Barry's world was the family farm and the hamlet of Perham. This was the world that nurtured and nourished his growth until adulthood. Though the environment itself was the same for all who lived there, the life of this lad of the land was different, as it is with all children. The green fields of spring colored in yellow struck a chord because years later when he thought of the dandelions of his childhood he would write of them. He just had to write his thoughts down, as he dreamed again of dirt and day lilies and dogs! The crystal stream down the road from his home first powered his interest in the brook trout that inhabited those clear waters. It was the beginnings of a life-long love affair with fishing. It was the multicolored fields of potato blossoms and oats and clover spread out together as a patch work quilt that shaped his love of the farm; he would one day simple call the "homestead." The northern skies of deep blue in the spring, the cruel blizzards of winter, the colored hills of fall, and the dry winds of summer molded and made him into a man that loves all seasons; made extra special when Rover was alive to enjoy those seasons with him.

CHILDHOOD

What was it that made this childhood worth remembering? Was it the simple Bible lessons taught Sunday after Sunday by a lady called Lily? (**"And that from a child thou hast known the holy scriptures, which are able to make thee wise unto salvation through faith which is in Christ Jesus"**—II Timothy 3:15) Was it the strict, but caring attitude of the teachers at the Perham Elementary School? Was it the games of Cowboys and Indians played with the Blackstone cousins and the McDougal brothers? Was it the furious apple fight he had in the old leaning barn across the road? Was it the hours spent in exploring the fields and forest surrounding the farm? Was it because Perham snow provided the best building material for either a snowman, or a snow fort? Was it the loving care received while laying home in bed with the mumps, or the measles? Was it the Friday night trips to Presque Isle to get groceries and visit Gramp and Gram Barton? Was it milking cows, feeding chickens, hoeing potatoes, (No, he knows it wasn't that!) raking hay, or spreading manure that made his childhood worth remembering? Maybe, it was simply a dog named Rover, and the many hours they spent together wandering and walking the homestead dreaming and scheming?

As Barry near his sixty-sixth birthday (March 6, 2017) and reflects on his early childhood in Perham, he realize even though he came into a world at war, he lived in a county at peace. Unlike so many children of today, he at least had a childhood, and not just any childhood, but a country childhood with a dog at his side. Solomon wrote: **"Therefore remove sorrow from thy heart, and put away evil from thy flesh: for childhood and youth are vanity!"** (Ecclesiastes 11:10) I don't know what kind of childhood Solomon had but it appears it wasn't a nice one; maybe, it was as simple as not having a dog named Rover? My childhood was anything but 'vanity' it was vital in making me what and who I am today!

DARKNESS

I WILL CONFESS TO you my abiding fear of certain dark places: confined dark places (like tunnels, caves, or huge rooms like a cow barn after dark, or cellar without a light) where there is little light or no light at all. What makes this so strange is my love of walking in the dark, in the evening; not inside, but outside, not indoors but out-of-doors. I love the experience, the wonder, the amazing sights that a walk at night holds. I first learned about these pleasant vistas and visions of the night while walking with my dog Rover on the Blackstone Homestead in Perham, Maine in the 1950s and early 1960s.

How can a man, who is afraid of the darkness, love the night? For me, it is the light that can be seen even at night; sights and sites that cannot be seen in the day, but can be spotted in the night. I am by my very nature draw to the light, any light. It doesn't have to be a big light; the only quality needed is that it sheds light on at least a small part of my world. Individually, a single star doesn't cast much light, but collectively, what a sight! My favorite nighttime light is the moon, in all its phases. I love a full moon, despite the frost it often brings with it in Northern Maine in the fall, winter, and spring months. It filled my world with a creamy color that brings contentment unmatched in the dark. A full moon often blocks out the starlight, but that light would return as the moon slowly lost its light. Even Rover liked to bark at the moon on our moonlight strolls!

Having been raised in the northern hemisphere, I have had the privilege to witness the aurora borealis in all of its glory, many times. Next to the moon, there can be no greater light show than a colorful aurora marking up an evening sky over the homestead. I still recall the first night my Dad called me out to the front porch

DARKNESS

to watch my first heavenly show. Without comment, we gazed in wonder at one of nature's greatest displays of light. All of nature seemed to fall silent in the majesty and magnificence of a horizon filled with giant searchlights streaking into the sky. If I am not mistaken even Rover stayed silent as we watched nature's laser show unfold that night!

Then there was my first falling star on a dark, black night. One of my favorite walking places in the evening was the Salmon Lake Road. Just a few hundred yards from my parent's home, the narrow gravel road was an ideal place to walk at night. No traffic, and open to the little light the heavens would yield, the road took you to a series of fields surrounded by forest. It was a warm mid-summer's eve, and the air was calm. The sky was clear and moonless, and the stars hadn't really come out yet in all their glory. I was walking that night just thinking. My dog Rover was by my side. He was looking for an occasional glimpse at a nocturnal animal; I was just looking upward at the heavenly bodies emerging from the blinding light of the sun. It was one of those night when you expected something to happen, but didn't really believe it, and then quite suddenly, it did.

It came in from the northwest, a small solid object streaking a brilliant tail of light across the sky. Its glory lasted but a few seconds as I gazed in wonder at my first falling star. Finally, as quick as it had appeared, it disappeared behind the tree line. I think Rover missed it because he never barked! Another example of things you can see in the dark that you can never see in the day! The Hebrews prophet Jeremiah used the imagery of darkness in this classic prophecy: **"Give glory to the Lord your God, before he cause darkness, and before your feet stumble upon the dark mountains, and, while ye look for light, He turn it into the shadow of death, and make it gross darkness."** (Jeremiah 13:16) Darkness can be deadly, dangerous, unless you look for the "light" in the darkness!

HEARTH

I live in a home with a hearth to this day. Just recently my wife asked if I would build her a fire in our living room fireplace. It was a cold winter's night and the extra warmth of wood heat felt inviting and comforting against the gathering subzero freeze outside. We watched television that evening in the glow of that fire and the heat from that hearth. Also that evening has reminded me of the many nights my boyhood family would gather around the hearth in our homestead home and one of the family members to enjoy the fire and the flames was my best friend 'Rover'.

My old homestead house had a great many rooms that were nearly all the same size. There was a kitchen with an old fashion appeal including water piped in from the barn well; a dining room with a well-worn table and chairs and a corner cupboard which held all of mother's treasures; a living room which contained an old radio in the corner, our only access to the outside world, especially in the winter months, and the last room on the first floor was the den which contained a piano and a fireplace; the hearth of our home. The four rooms on the first floor where matched almost perfectly with four large bedrooms upstairs. With each room having nine and a half foot ceilings, the house was massive and difficult to heat with only a small wood stove in the kitchen and a larger wood stove in the basement for the rest of the house. Gravity was the only means to get the heat around, so the fireplace in the den would often come in handy on those extra frigid January nights.

It was at this fireplace that I spent many an evening with my sister, Sylvia, playing games in the flickering light from the hearth. I enjoyed the pleasure of lying flat upon the floor and gazing into the brilliant embers created by the burning logs. Its memory still

HEARTH

inspires me to see the faces reflected in the glow of that pile of burning maple as I ponder the importance of the hearth. Rover would often be found lying beside me; for only on the coldest nights would mother allow Rover to come into the den from the kitchen. Mother was not a dog loves, or a cat loves, but Rover was the only animal that must have touched her heart because Rover is the only animal I remember in my boyhood to have been invited into the house, let alone into the den, but only on wintery nights!

As I gazed into those crackling fagots, I would dream of great things and read of even greater tales of adventure and war. It was resting on that old hearth that I developed a love for fireside meditation. Who was the criminal that banished the hearth from the modern home? Who was the vandal that removed the hearth from the modern house? Who was the outlaw that outlawed the hearth from the modern family? Perhaps, this is one of the reasons the family is in such disarray today. The dear old fireplace has been replaced by an impersonal furnace in the cellar, a heat pump in the living room. The inspiring old hearth has been replaced by the uninspiring computer in the corner. The lovely old fireside has been replaced by the entertainment center in the middle of the game room. We have lost a wonderful scene of comfort that comes from a dog sleeping by a fire, and an even more important source of conversation!

I have never forgotten the lessons of the hearth; the importance of conversation, inspiration, and imagination. I have with me today the produce of the hearth; togetherness, stillness, and lovingkindness. To this day that old hearth generates a vivid vision of a day long passed when a fire could not only heat the body, but warm the soul! Even the Hebrew prophet Isaiah speaks of the " . . . **fire from the hearth . . .** " (Isaiah 30:14)

WISH

It's funny to me how 'a wish' changes as life changes! When I was a young boy living with my best friend Rover, I often wished I would become a famous baseball player for the Boston Red Sox, or a well-known basketball star with the Celtics. (I was then and I am still to this day a fan of all New England sports teams; Go Patriots-written just before the greatest Super Bowl comeback in history!) Even later into my high school years, I imagined living far away from the farm, and saw myself a world traveler doing important things especially in the area of soldiering for Uncle Sam. I wished away my childhood transporting myself to distant battlefields as a heroic soldier. Despite the fact I lived in an era when the homestead was at its best, I still missed its brilliant beauty, its colorful countryside, and its shining sod. Not one of my boyhood wishes came true, and as I pass into old-age, I fear many of my adult wishes won't either; like seeing my son live to forty! (When I was in my 3rd pastorate I had a deacon that told me never to make a final verdict on my children's lives until they passed 40. That might have been good advice for some parents and their children, but my boy died at 39 from lung and liver cancer!)

I got a call the other day (in the 1990s) from my brother, the homestead brother, the last Blackstone owner of the farm. In the process of the conversation, I asked how things were going on the farm. He shared the dismal forecast that after the cows left the homestead the year before now it looked like the potato crop would be the next to go. If financing couldn't be found this year (it wasn't), a 134-year old working, farming operation would stop functioning. Since that call, I have done a lot of wishing.

I wish I could spend one more winter on the old homestead; a snowy, stormy winter with great heaps of snow and howling,

WISH

wild winds. To feel again the heavy wool cloths that protected me from the sub-zero temperature as I walked to the barn to take care of the calves of spring; to build again the potato house fires; too slid one more time down the driveway with sister Sylvia; to build one more snow fort with cousin Clayton; to make one more snow angel with cousin Dale, and to have one more homestead snowball fight with cousin Doug, and to walk again in the snow with a dog called Rover.

I wish I could spend one more spring on the old homestead; a warm, colorful spring with plenty of dandelions. To watch again as the green grass takes over the drab pasture land; to fix fence and harrow fields dry and ready for spring planting; to help Dad dump barrel after barrel of seed into the old potato planter along with bag after bag of fertilizer; to ride one more time over that old lane that leads to the Paul Place with Rover, and to see the first ground hog of the year poke his head out of his burrow!

I wish I could spend one more summer on the old homestead; a hot, but cool summer, a damp but dry summer. To walk again through knee deep clover; to go fishing with my Cousins Dale and Bob to Beaver Brook; to sweat once more in the top rafters of the great cow barn as the last bale of hay is stored away for winter; and to hear Rover's bark echo again off the front of the massive cow barn near my homestead house!

I wish I could spend one more autumn on the old homestead; an Indian summer fall with a perfect harvesting season. To smell again dying potato tops, while picking apples in Gramp's apple orchard; to see the leaves change into brilliant reds and oranges along the ridges behind the Russell Place; to roll a potato barrel on a moving truck; to throw the grapples over one more barrel of Katahdins; to walk once more with my boyhood dog among the leaves of Autumn, and to put my arms around Rover's neck and thank him for being the best dog a boy could have ever had!

But now I see the only good 'wish' is the one invoked by the Apostle John in his third epistle when he wished: **"Beloved, I wish above all things that thou mayest prosper and be in health, even as thy soul prospereth."** (III John 2) Amen and Amen!

SWING

THIS PAST SPRING I hung a 'board swing' in a front yard Maple tree of the parsonage of the Emmanuel Baptist Church for my daughter Marnie. Marnie loves to swing. Though I don't remember any such tree swings from my childhood that doesn't mean I never had a swing, and that doesn't mean that Rover wasn't around while I was swinging!

When you are raised on a working potato/dairy farm there wasn't much time for play, but there was time. There wasn't much time for parents and kids to play together, but there was play. I was very fortunate to be raised with a lot of male cousins (Clayton, Dale, David, Doug, Gary, and of course Bob) and a few good neighbors (Morris and Steven). We pretty much were on our own when it came to making our own fun. We were poor and times were tough according to the standards of today, but back in the 1950's and 1960's, we thought we were ok; even well-to-do. With a little imagination and a length of rope and a dog, (Rover wasn't much of a swinger, but he loved to bark while the rest of us took a turn) a swing wasn't hard at all to make.

My boyhood swing was a 'barn swing'. There were plenty of trees around my home on the Russell Place, but seemingly none with a good branch for a swing. Where branches were limited, barn beams were plentiful. A length of rope over a lower beam tied to an old tire would give me an excellent swing. The lower beams would limit how high you could go, but on a rainy day with little to do on the homestead, a good swing in the tire could take you just about any place your imagination could carry you. I still can smell the fresh cut clover that had been stored in the lower haymows. Of course, as the summer progressed, and the haying increased, I would lose my lower swinging area, but that was ok because I

SWING

would only move my swing to a higher beam and Rover would get more excited as his master became more daring.

A four story barn was located just across the driveway from my home, so needless to say I spent a lot of time in that barn. Eight and ten inch timbers formed the cross beams in the structure, and as I grew older the more adventurous I became! My swing went higher and higher into the hayloft. Sometimes I would leave the tire off and only make a large knot at the end of my swing. If attached to one of the middle beams, the swing could be up to twenty feet. Once a hay pile was created at one end of the barn, a swing and jump was possible. Starting from a second story platform, the "swinger" could 'fly through the air with the greatest of ease' until he let go to land in a thick pile of freshly cut hay. It was the closest I ever got to flying in my childhood. And with each swing Rover would race back and forth; I think he thought he was my 'spotter'!

Swings were for solitude, but they were also for social interaction. My swing often drew a crowd, especially my dog Rover. What we could think to do on those old swings. I have seen a cousin or two, with a neighbor or two pushing another cousin so hard that they nearly wrap themselves around the beam. The swing you couldn't create on your own was easily created by a few willing assistants as they pushed you to greater heights. Sometimes we miss calculated the weight on the rope and the swing broke, or the tension on the tire and the rope came undone, but despite the many hard falls, and the rope burns, I don't ever remember not getting up and retying and returning to a summer of swingin'. As I write this article " **. . . summer is now nigh at hand . . .** " (Luke 21:30), but two things will be missing from this summer: my childhood swing and my boyhood dog! Both are now just a remembrance of 'the good old summertime' of my youth!

ROADSIDE

I HAVE RETURNED AGAIN alone from one of my long walks along the Union River. It is early autumn in coastal Maine. It is also my favorite time for walking and watching what goes on along the roadsides as I walk. Each trip up the Mills Highways causes me to reminisce just a bit to the days when my roadside wasn't next to the lanes of Hancock County, but the fields on my family's farm along the back roads of Aroostook County and I didn't walk alone then, for Rover was there.

For countless years now, I have harbored a guilt because I did not properly appreciate the homestead I lived on for nearly twenty years. Now when I return and see what time and tough potato years has caused to the farm and my family, I realize that change and circumstance will never allow me to walk by those roadsides again. I missed the best years on the farm because I was too busy hurrying off to nowhere. I so quickly passed through that all I have left of the roadsides of my youth are a few passing glances stored away in my homestead memory. And so I won't forget them or Rover again, I will write them down that one day when the memory fades I will recall them through these stories.

I remember green lawns for as far as I could see. We are not talking about golf course lawns, but the All-American lawn. Around every building and barn was a piece of the farm solely set aside for my mowing! Maybe that was the reason I didn't notice. My Grandmother and Uncle came for a visit the other day and one of our conversations was about mowing the lawns on the farm. My Uncle Paul has just retired from a job in New Jersey and has resettled back to the homestead. Besides talking care of my ninety-two year old grandmother (she would live into her 100th year), he has become the unofficial caretaker of the homestead lawns. For

ROADSIDE

the job, he bought a forty-eight inch cut lawn tractor. I remember when I pushed instead of rode. (Postscript: eight years ago my Uncle Paul died and left my grandmother's house to me. I am once again mowing the lawns of one of the first paying jobs I had in my youth.) I don't ever remember riding, but the view from the roadside was beautiful, especially when Rover was there.

I remember green woods for as far as I could see. We lived on the back side of Perham next to the Northern Maine Woods. But the forest that surrounded the fields of Perham was always beautiful. Whether covered in the brilliant colors of autumn, or the white snow of winter, the woods along my boyhood paths were like a Norman Rockwell painting. Mixed with dandelions in the spring or clover in the summer, the combination of sight and savor along the roadside was a nature lover's paradise. And what I liked about those roadsides Rover seemed to enjoy as well, for often when I couldn't go for a walk he was off alone, as I am today, for a stroll along the roadways of Perham.

I remember green fields for as far as I could see. The homestead was dotted with small field created by the strong backs and broad shoulders of my ancestors. Each field had a road or a lane getting to it. Even witch grass, pigweed, barn grass, and mustard plants looked good against the back drop of hay fields and potato fields and oat fields. I wish I would have relaxed more, and enjoyed more my days and years walking and riding and working on the homestead with Rover along the roadsides of my early life. My Old King James Bible only used the word 'road' once in its text and it is found in a question: " ... **Whither have ye made a road to day? ...** " (I Samuel 27:10) I didn't know it then, but I realize it now that despite not taking advantage of my opportunities to spend more times in the roadside I have created in my memory bank many a road down memory lane!

WINDOW

I LOVE TO LOOK out windows. I have my recliner setting in our living room at the parsonage of the Emmanuel Baptist Church in Ellsworth, Maine so I can look out the window. Often when television begins to question my intelligence, I simply turn my head and begin to gaze upon the out-of-doors which has never bored me. The view from my window has changed over the years, but no matter, for the more I watch television the more I turn from that window to the world, to the window overlooking my world, and I like what I see through my window best. With the world falling, failing, and faltering fast I find more pleasure in the past than in the present. With all that is on TV now, murder, misery, and mayhem, it would do us all good to look out our windows a little more often, especially if there is a dog on the other side. (The dog I most see today is a small lad named Mauritius, a neighbor's dog who thinks my cat Eddie is his best friend; Eddie not so much?) When I was a boy the dog I saw most out my window was Rover!

I don't remember how old I was when I first looked out through my bedroom window in my parent's house onto our homestead in Perham, Maine, but I do remember what I saw. Before me, within the confines of my window, lay the sum told of my world as a child. In the wee hours of the morning, the barnyard looked like a ghost town out of the old west, but as the sun rose over the eastern hills it came alive. The first thing I would see would be my Dad's old 1947 green International pickup driving into the dooryard returning from morning chores at the old Milking Shed about a mile through the Sugar Woods; which I could see out of the corner of my eye to my right. Amidst the sun shining in my eyes I could see my dog Rover meeting Dad as he stops; then I watched both of them enter the huge cow barn next to the farmhouse to do the

WINDOW

morning chores there. How Rover liked to be a part of the action, even if it was work. But within the framework of my second story bedroom window were many other things to see.

Up the road I could see our neighbor's house, the McDougall's. The large family lived in a small two story house with a wood shed on the back. Mr. McDougall worked for the State of Maine, and his wife made the best butter I ever tasted. They keep a few cows in a falling down old barn which I could barely see from my window. Emma would separate the buttermilk and hand churn the butter from the milk. On homemade bread or biscuits, the two would produce a favor unmatched, and as you can see unforgettable. Often my best friend Morris would be the first to appear in the McDougall's yard, and I would know it was my sign to get dressed and hurry out to play. Our play would often include games within the confines of the wood to my left as I peered through my window. We had paths, secret and otherwise, that crisscrossed between his house, the old pickers shack, our car garage, which was located across the road, and the old set of farm building located down the road and behind my window. Of course, Rover was a constant companion as we travelled through the maze of forest trails. I have just closed the blinds on that window from my past, but I dare say that I will probably open it again.

Over my years as a pastor I have discovered that the Bible also speaks often of *'windows'* both symbolically and literally. Moses spoke of 'the windows of heaven' (Genesis 7:11, 8:2) opening as a 40-day rain flooded Noah's world! Noah would build one window into the ark, and would use that window to release the birds (Genesis 8:6) that would check on the waters drying up. David (I Samuel 19:12) and Paul (II Corinthians 11:33) would escape through windows. The best is found in Malachi 3:10; check it out and find one of the best promises found in Holy Writ!

TEARS

IT HAS BEEN NEARLY four months since I sat at my computer to capture another Rover memory. Spring was in full bloom when I recalled my last remembrance, but tomorrow fall comes and much has happened to our old homestead, Rover's old stomping grounds. This was the first summer since 1861 that a member of my family didn't work the potato ground of the ancient farm. I returned to the sacred sod twice this summer, but all I felt was sadness. It was the driest summer on record, but that didn't mean water didn't fall, for there were plenty of wet tears for the passing of a family's heritage and homestead legacy: much like the day when Rover passed away and Gramp passed; the only three times I remember shedding a tear on the homestead, but will there be more (there was!).

I will never forget setting with my mother around the kitchen table as she explained to me her feeling of my brother's decision to no longer farm. The more she talked the more the tears flowed. I didn't fully understand our hurt until I received a letter from my pastor cousin (Clayton) from Idaho the other day. He too had been home for the summer, and had felt the tears. In his letter he told me as he was flying back home to his parish, he had read these words from the pen of Michael Phillips and Judith Pella. They hit home: "To man's undiscerning eye, the generations come and go, fading one into the other, ultimately passing from the face of the earth. As the march of history progresses, ONLY THE LAND REMAINS, while men, women and children grow, live, and die and then return to the earth from which they came, seemingly swallowed into nothingness by a vast, uncaring universe... In reality, however, the land is the stage upon which the drama of unparalleled eternal significance is played within the hearts of every man and woman who sets foot upon it . . . Twentieth century mentality is often based on the present; we live in a vacuum of now. Yet every life is the result of a series of choices and crossroads . . . not only ours, but those of our ancestors for the generations behind us. In the present, as in the past, each individual holds a key to the future. We stand at the crossroad of our personal histories, and the decisions we make set into motion values and attitudes that affect not only our own development as men and women made in the image of God, but the choices and decisions that will face our descendants for generations to come." The Blackstones had come once again to another homestead crossroad! Tears have been shed over decisions that no Blackstone living in or outside the borders of the homestead could have altered; caught up in the political and economic realities of this year, two young Blackstone cousins made a decision that will affect all four Blackstone generations now living. "Perhaps," as my dear cousin from Idaho thoughtfully ended his letter, **"One of those who follow us will strike it rich and restore the homestead to its heyday?"** (One has but he will not!) I have had the same hope, but till our tears of sadness are turned to tears of joy, we mourn the loss with a Blackstone Homestead tear! Even if the farm is restored, one aspect of its heyday will never return and that is the bark of a dog named 'Rover', or a grandfather named Carroll. According to the Bible there is only one place " . . . God will wipe away all tears from their eyes . . . " (Revelation 7:17, 21:4) Though I wrote the bulk of this article back in the 1990s, I am compiling this series of memories of Rover in 2017. Over the last two years Amish families from Western Pennsylvania have been buying up pieces of the homestead and returning the farmland back to dairy land. This might be the year I sell my piece, but as with Gramp, Rover, and the end of the Blackstone farm in Blackstone hands, I will be surprise if a few tears are not shed. (Many tears were shed when on a May Day in 2017 we buried grandfather (Wendell) and grandson (Scott) on the same day in the family burial plot on the Blackstone Road overlooking our ancestral home!)

SCHOOL

This morning I took my kids (Scott and Marine) to school; as I have for most of their elementary education. It is only a two and one half mile trip to a private church school on the outskirts of Ellsworth, Maine. As I drove home however, I slipped back thirty years into my past to a time when my sister and I waited by the roadside with our dog Rover; to be picked up by George Harris in his small yellow school bus. The trip to our four-room country school was more of a journey than a ride, and this morning I took that journey again, but I am afraid Rover had to be left beside the driveway.

As my mind retraced that old bus route fond recollections enshrined in the temple of my memory began to flood back. We made our way down the hill and across Salmon

Brook as we headed toward Tangle Ridge. A lot of water has run down that creek since the last time I crossed that stream in an old yellow school bus. With each stop the bus filled with old neighbors and good friends; I must admit, I haven't thought about in years. As we made our way through the woods around Tangle Ridge I lingered in those gentler and simpler days when the conversations were clean and the kids were kind (I don't remember one bully!). Then after an hour of storytelling and fellowship we drove into the Perham Elementary School yard reacquainted and ready for a day of learning and living.

I know that little four teacher school building has long since burned, and for an even longer time was turned into an apartment building, but for me it will always be my country school and school yard (actually a simple trailer sets on the lot today). Eight grades of country kids who didn't have much, know much, or want much, yet they made much to do of their school. We were the Perham

SCHOOL

Pirates and we were very proud of it. I remember the rooms were placed in counter clockwise order so as you moved from room to room you were climbing a ladder of achievement. For the first two years (no kindergarten then) you were in Mrs. Conroy's room. Then it was Mrs. Beverage's third and fourth grade room. Being on the left side of the hall you were at the bottom of the rung, but when you crossed the hall into Mr. Humphrey's room, and finally into Mr. Harper's room you had arrived. You had gone as far in Perham as you could go. You were an eighth grader and you had attained something. Those were the days when you had good health and a good healthy respect for teachers. An hour at noon was spent in playful fun not smoking, or shooting up. We learned the basic of reading and writing and arithmetic with history and geography and spelling explained. We were not hampered with SATs and Colorado placement tests, computers or other gadgets. We grew and learned in a wholesome place with plain ordinary people as our guide and instructors.

The decades have passed, and my old country school and that old gang of mine have long since dispersed and a few have passed, just like Rover. I am passed fifty (nearly 66 as I compile these remembrances of Rover), but I am still in school. I'm afraid I am a slow learner and will never make magna cum laude, but I have not dropped out, for if I learned anything in my little boyhood schoolhouse it was to finish my day's work, get on the bus, and go home to a waiting dog (now a cat)! There is only one school mentioned in the Bible: " . . . the school of one Tyrannus . . . " (Acts 19:9), and as far as I am concerned there was really only one school in my childhood. I would go on to Washburn District High School and Bob Jones University, but neither of them had a dog waiting when I returned home from school. Rover died while I was attending Perham Elementary and coming home from school never was really the same again!

PORCH

WHAT EVER HAPPENED TO the house porch? You don't see them much anymore, especially in the city. I think they ought to make a porch a requirement for a new house. You show me an old house and I'll show you a porch; that is unless they have boarded it in, or tore it off. I am fortunate where I live now to have an old fashion porch on my house; filled with hanging plants, flower boxes, porch furniture, and a swing. Despite my folks closing in one porch, and abandoning another on their home in Perham, Maine I still have some marvelous memories about a porch and a dog named Rover.

Often as the sun sets and the day draws to a close, you will find me setting on the front porch of our home in Ellsworth, Maine, remembering. The old, open ended porch has become a favorite stopping off place, for from there I can easily think back. It is a short trip because of the days I spent on my parent's porch when I was a little lad. It was from that porch I could get a good look at my world. From that platform I watched my dog Rover chase cats in the barnyard, and witness the plight of a crow being attacked by a squadron of sparrows because he had come to close to a sparrow's nest. It was from that porch that Rover and I started most of our adventures. The porch lead to the lawn, and for a barefoot boy there is nothing more thrilling than to feel tall grass sliding through his toes; anyone for a run, a stroll maybe, or just a walk with your dog?

I am afraid the house porch is a relic from an age far removed in our society. I was fortunate to have lived in a day and place were the television and the air-conditioner hadn't discovered Perham, so the porch was a favorite gathering place on a hot and humid summer's night. In those days the porch was a necessity, not a novelty. It was a gathering place for people and for dogs, not a

PORCH

collection place for possessions, a storage unit. For me a house has to have three things to make it a home: you need a porch for the summer months and a fireplace for the winter months, and a dog to lie in front of them both! Instead of homes becoming places where families are brought together, we are simply creating fueling stations, and sleeping places. Our culture has stopped bringing people together, and we are the losers for it; why the need of dogs and porches.

    I can still see my sister and I playing games on the front porch will Mum and Dad talked of the day that had passed. I remember people coming by just to "sit a spell", and "talk a while". I recall the light shows the fireflies would put on in the summer twilight, and the northern lights in the winter. They all could be seen from the porch. Oh, there were the times when the black flies and mosquitoes would drive you inside, but the crickets and bullfrogs would call you back out the next night. I like what Donna Christian once wrote about a porch. **"It is still a nice place to tell a story or read one; to listen to music or play some; to frolic with your children or be one."** And don't forget Donna, a place to play with your dog! I was the minister at my youngest sister's wedding on the front porch of my parent's house; now that's the way to start a marriage!

    By now you must have realized if the Bible speaks of something I am convinced it either is a good something that should be extolled and exhorted, or a bad something what should be rebuked and reproved! In one of the greatest structures of ancient man, Herod, the builder of the Jerusalem Temple, added a 'porch'; Solomon's porch (Acts 3:11). In the famous miracle at the Pool of Bethesda, it speaks of it having 'five porches' (John 5:2). It was on 'a porch' (Matthew 26:71, Make 14:68) that Peter the infamous cock crow. Today it is a parsonage porch and a cat named Eddie, but 'once upon a time'!

HIKER

IF YOU HAVE DONE much hiking then you have discovered that the greatest pleasures are in the challenge of the climb, the difficulty of the trail, and the strain and stress of the hike. Hikers are not content with strolling the level roadways reserved for walkers. To simply walk on the straight and level is a bore to a hiker. The goal of the hiker is to reach higher ground, and if that ground is covered in snow, then better the trip. And if that hike is shared with a dog named Rover than better still!

    I lived in the hilly section of Aroostook County in Northern Maine. Oh, there is some flatland in 'the county', but not where I lived. Hill and hallows would better describe my family farm, so scaling heights and tackling ridges were what I did as a child. I wanted **"to scale the utmost height and catch a gleam of glory bright"** to the summit of everything, God-made or man-made. Granted, there were no mountains or high-country on the homestead, but there were a few places that took some vigor of spirit to conquer, that is if you were just a kid. I was fortunate also to have parents that thought it was normal for a young lad to explore his world with his dog. (I think they thought that Rover would be my protector, but in the Perham of my childhood there was little I needed to be protected from.) Strenuous was not a bad thing, but an everyday part of a working dairy and potato farm. Nothing was easy in the 1950's and 1960's on a Maine farm. It took a discipline of both mind and muscle to get the farm work done. It took fortitude and fight to accomplish the task of hand picking the potato crop. It took strength and stamina to get in the annual hay harvest. Hiking was just a part of the training needed to perform normal barnyard tasks, especially when you had a companion to encourage you upward.

HIKER

Rover and I's first memorable hike was to the top of the hill overlooking my hometown of Perham. From the summit of the knoll on the Blackstone Road you could gaze into the hamlet of Perham, the village of Washburn, and the city of Caribou. On a clear day you could see the boundaries of my boyhood world. The autumn is upon us here on the coast of Maine and the fall foliage is at its peak, but nothing to be compared to the view from atop that hill in Perham. Hiking gets you a better view!

Our second memorable hike was to the top of the ridge visible from my bedroom window. On the way up the very steep hill I had to pass my neighbor's house. Often Morris, another boyhood friend, would climb that hill with us. Sometimes we would stay on the road that also climbed the hill, but many times we would take the wood's path. Climbing and hiking through forest is much more difficult than a roadway, but the rewards are worth the extra effort. As we slowing climbed the ridge, we could hear the birds as they protested our invasion of their domain. Hiking gets you a better sound!

Our third memorable hike was to the top of the knoll overlooking Salmon Lake. Over a mile from home, the small hill had been cleared for farming. Despite it being a working place, it became our quiet spot. I went there often to think and pray and ponder life's questions. Hiking gets you a better perspective on life! Hiking is all about pressing " . . . **toward the mark for the prize . . .** " (Philippians 3:14) One of the earliest Church hymns I learned to sing was Johnson Oatman, Jr. classic song "Higher Ground". I have already quoted a line in this article, but you need to hear a few more to understand my theology of hiking with Rover: **"I'm pressing on the upward way, new heights I'm gaining every day; still praying as I'm onward bound, 'Lord, plant my feet on higher ground."** My childhood hiking was just an earthly experience into a heavenly calling that one day will be fulfilled when I walk 'the golden streets' (Revelation 21:21)

SLEEP

WHEN YOU ARE RAISED on a hard, working farm, sleep was an important part of your life. To endure the tasks of an active dairy and potato homestead, rest was essential as you worked from sunrise to sunset, especially during the spring, summer, and fall. I learned very early in life from the example of my dog Rover and my Dad that to enjoy work, a Blackstone Homestead sleep was just what the doctor, or Dad, or dog ordered!

I learned how to sleep from the masters, Rover and Dad. They could sleep anywhere. I have pictures of Rover sleeping with his head propped against an old blanket in the corner of the kitchen by the pantry door. I can still see in my mind's eye Rover resting against a tire of his Model "G" John Deer tractor during a noon time nap in a potato field as Dad slept on the seat. Rover's favorite place to rest was in the woodshed at the foot of the stairs. After a hearty lunch, Rover could be to asleep within seconds of laying his head down, while dad slept on the couch in the living room. Though I never perfected the amazing speed by which Rover and Dad could get to sleep, I too had my favorite spots.

The first I recall was the stoop in the bay window that uses to be located in the dining room of my childhood home. The huge window, especially large when you are just a little lad, opened up to the backyard of our home. Sunday afternoons at the Blackstone house were for resting, that is until it was time to go milk the cows. After the biggest meal of the week, it was nice to curl up in that sunny spot and it seemed to only take minutes to drop off to sleep. The combination of a full stomach and the warm rays of the sun are still the best sleeping pill in the world for me. I always hated to hear Dad's call to chores when I was sleeping in the bay window with my hand on my black and white dog.

SLEEP

The next place I remember for sleeping was our cow barn. Nestled between two bales of straw using your jacket as a pillow, what times of rest I had. Naps could be taken when I waited for the next load of hay to come from the field. Another time of rest was during lunch hour. Instead of returning home for a meal, many times Mum would bring our meals to us, especially during the busy time of haying. Lunch was not the only time, but supper was also served when there was more hay to get in than time to get it in. A power nap would provide the energy to finish piling that last load of hay. And then there were times, when things were slow, not too often, but times when nobody was around and you felt a little tired that you could go into the haymow and just sink into a pile of loose hay and sleep the afternoon away. I still love to sleep in the afternoon (the best time for me), I wonder if it isn't because of those naps in the hayloft with Rover?

Sleep is something many today don't seem to get much of. Perhaps the reason is they never learned the joy of sleeping where they are. A comfortable spot in a sunny or shady place is all that is required for a good sleep, and of course a good dog! As I grew into adulthood I forgot the lessons of Rover and my father, how my Dad could nap. Only when I realized that sleep was one of God's great gifts to mankind did I understand the spiritual significance of sleep: " . . . **for He giveth His beloved sleep."** (Psalm 127:2) As I have grown older I have come to realize that I need more sleep, not less! In my twenties, I would work on about six hours of rest, but no more. I need nine or ten now to be fully functional even in my low energy job as a pastor. That is why I love this proverb by the wise man Solomon: **"When thou liest down, thou shalt not be afraid: yes, thou shalt lie down, and thy sleep shall be sweet!"** (Proverbs 3:24) So take it from the Scriptural statute on sleep, and if that isn't enough just check out your pet and see how often they sleep!

DOOR

As I near sixty-six I find myself going back in my mind to the old homestead in the hills. It is winter here on the coast of Maine, and despite the season I have only pleasant thoughts of the house of my childhood. Today, I am thinking of its doors and the dog I went in and out of them with.

The first remembrances of the doors of my boyhood are that **they were all unlocked**. I don't remember any keys in my youth. Today, I carry such a string of keys that I walk sideways because of the weight. No keys in my boyhood. I was never locked out once, or locked in. For most of my adulthood (mother and father sold the old house about five years ago) I could unexpectedly arrive at the home place and find the doors all unlocked. I wonder if mum or dad knew where any of the keys to house where anyway?

As I stroll through the doors of my youth, I recall that each had a welcome mate (figuratively speaking-I don't remember any actual mates) in front of them. There wasn't a door that had a sign saying 'stay out' on it. My parents never locked their bedroom door and neither were the doors of any of the bedrooms locked. I was as free to wander into my sister's room as she was mine. Granted, that wouldn't go over today, but I don't remember any troubles over it in my day. Friends walked in and out with the freedom of a family member. You have to remember that in those days all neighbors were friends and those that weren't, stayed to themselves, and 'Rover' was no guard dog because we never need any kind of guard on the doors of my boyhood!

I remember the doors of my youth as bring exits to wonderful worlds of adventure. To open a door was to open a window. The world of my boyhood was a playground filled with excitement and fun. Often my best friend 'Rover' was on the other side of the door

DOOR

waiting my arrival. Sometimes it was my neighbor Morris waiting my exit from lunch or chores. The other side of the door, depending on the season, one could found snow or sunshine, rain or robins. Sometimes it was the friendly faces of my cousins that waited my return to the out-of-doors; whether somebody or nobody, the other side of the door was Rover and my favorite side of the door.

My mind still sees each of the doors of my childhood. I see the kitchen door that lead to the pantry and the pantry door that lead to the woodshed and the woodshed door that lead to the barnyard. The woodshed door is now a garage door, but in the memory of this 66 year old, I have made no structural changes to the old place. The basement door lead to an old rock lined cellar. The hall door led to the staircase to the second floor. The attic door lead to a treasure house of articles in the upstairs, and the porch door lead to a marvelous setting place in the summer. Then there were the barn doors and the tool shed doors and the potato house doors and the milking room doors. Not to forget the grange shed doors and the door to my grandparent's house and the doors to my uncle's homes. Then there were the stable doors and the chicken coup doors. As I can see now I spend most of my boyhood opening and shutting doors, but all made pleasant in the early years by a dog named Rover who also liked going through doors. He was not a good shutter!

The Bible talks about 'doorkeepers': **"For a day in Thy court is better than a thousand. I had rather be a doorkeeper in the house of my God, than to dwell in the tents of wickedness."** (Psalm 84:10) As I look back on my past, I realize that I was blessed to walk through the doors and doorways of my youth. They were not barred doors, closed doors, or dangerous doors. They were the exits and entrances into a wonderful life!

WILDERNESS

When I was a lad, Rover and I lived on the edge of a wonderful and wild wilderness. I can still hear my father said, **"If you enter the woods from behind the cow barn, the next stop will be Quebec City, Canada!"** Granted, you would have needed to across Route 11 somewhere around Ashland, but after that: the Alagash Wilderness, the border with Canada, and the waters of the St. Lawrence were the only obstacles separating you from Quebec, Canada. However, when I was a boy that wilderness was still inviting and interesting, exciting and entertaining when you roamed with a boyhood friend!

It seemed that no matter where you were on the Blackstone homestead you were not very far from the woods. The edge of my wilderness surrounded every field of the 720 area dairy/potato farm. Even the cow pastures and the meadows in the back part of the farm were on the edge of the wilderness known as "The Great Northern Maine Woods!" Today, it is only woods, but in my childhood, "wilderness" was a better description of this region Rover and I explored together in my boyish years.

There were bear in my wilderness, the famous Maine Black Bear. I only remember seeing a few, but I always saw that they were around. I still recall the first time Dad took me into the wilderness to see the bones of a dead Holstein the bears had picked clean. I still remember the times while picking berries the mowed down areas where the bears had feasted. I am still reminded of the walks along the oat fields in the fall, and the areas where the bears had feed on Blackstone grain. One of the biggest thrills of my boyhood (though I regret it to this day, for I would rather see a wild animal alive in the woods than as a trophy on a wall!) was the day I shot my only bear with Dad's Thirty/Thirty rifle. I am not proud of it

WILDERNESS

now, but in the wilderness of Perham it was the crowning experience of my short hunting career. If I remember correctly Rover wasn't there to see it, for Rover didn't have a killer spirit and I think he would have been ashamed of mine then!

There were plenty of rabbits and partridge and porcupines and squirrels in our wilderness. A trip into the woods would always expose one or more of these creatures.

The birds of the forest were plenteous as well, so the utterances of the woodland were pleasant noises, not scary sounds to me; besides I had Rover. The hoot of the owls, the chatter of the squirrels, and the songs of the songbirds was always worth a stop in the wilderness just to listen. Many of these voices have been silenced with chemicals and logging and buckshot, but those that remain still lead me home, called be back for another stroll along the edge of the wilderness with a dog called 'Rover'.

There were white-tail deer and Bull Moose in my childhood wilderness as well. Much like the bear, they were more often than not seen in what they left, but the rare glimpse of them bounding out of sight was exciting every time. It was their footprints in the mud, or the snow off the back lanes of the homestead that first announced their presence. You could find a tree where they had rubbed, or their droppings where here and there. Added to these signs was the hawk in a big pine and wild geese sightings high overhead. One of my favorites was the fox. Catching one of them in an opening was also rare, but worth any trip to the edge of the wilderness with Rover. The Psalmist often spoke of the 'wilderness' in his psalms, and there are at least 20 named 'wildernesses' mentioned in the Bible; like, "the wilderness of Beersheba" (Genesis 21:14), "the wilderness of Gibeon" (II Samuel 2:24), and the "wilderness of Ziph" (I Samuel 23:14). It has only hit me recently that Rover and I lived in the Wilderness of Perham!

STROLL

OCTOBER IS PARTRIDGE (I Samuel 26:20) hunting season in Maine. It is also the most beautiful time in the year to take a stroll into the Great North Woods in my opinion. It is another Friday night in the city of Ellsworth, and I long for the days when Friday meant the freedom to go bird hunting with my dog Rover. School was over and a stroll into the back pastures of the homestead looking for nature's finest meat (Jeremiah 17:11) was homework I didn't mind doing, especially, if Rover went along for the hunt.

By the time I reached middle school, I was an avid bird hunter (I had not yet gotten a full taste of fishing or the ills of hunting; both would happen in my twenties). With plenty of woods on my family's farm in Perham, Maine, the opportunity for hunting was behind every building and out every door. Dad had taught me to hunt at a very early age, so it wasn't strange upon getting home from classes at Perham Elementary to grab the old four ten shotgun and a few shells and take a jaunt into the forest behind the cow barn with my favorite bird dog. A road leading to a back hay pasture was usually my first destination. A number of apple trees lined that old trail, and partridge love apples. In my mind I see myself walking slowly through the cow pasture heading for that private path. As I walk, I am carried back to a gentler generation and a sweeter season in Perham, if not the world. I was not out necessarily to kill a game bird, but to witness once again the stillness of the spruce. Within minutes, I was enough in the woods to quiet the few car sounds that would pass my homestead home. I had made my escape into the sanctuary of my boyhood and a stroll with my dog Rover all wrapped up in one excursion.

With every step I laid aside the accumulated burdens of the week. Our pace slowed to a crawl lest we pass supper hiding

STROLL

under a fur branch. Our vision checked every movement to make sure it wasn't a plump partridge trying to get out of my line of fire. Our ears strained to hear every sound. Our senses were alert, but my mind was drifting. Deep down I dreamed the dreams of a boy heading towards teenage hood, and not knowing what I would do, or what I would become. My strolls into the back fields of my mind were as productive as the strolls into the back fields with Rover. Strolling gave a twelve year old a chance to think, away from the distraction of a family of five, soon to be seven, the expectation of parents, and the anticipation of grandparents. **Bang!** But never to diverted to get a partridge setting exposed on the limb of an crab apple tree.

As we make our way around the Russell Place and the field we had just finished digging a few days ago, I thought again of the insane world I was growing up in. My nation was at war in a far-off and distant Vietnam, the Cuban Missile Criss, and the threat of all out nuclear war with Russia was on my mind and the minds of my generation. But in a back field on my beloved farm I was away from the "maddening crowd's ignoble strife". The only war here was between bird and boy and dog. How simple it seemed. How uncomplicated, as Rover and I finished our stroll with one less shell!

The whole journey took an hour, as did the writing of its memory. I have been challenged often to write by this instruction to John before he wrote the Revelation: **"Write the things which thou hast seen, and the things which are . . . "** (Revelation 1:19) Much has changed since those days, and the major difference is I no longer stroll or hunt with Rover. But this one thing hasn't changed and that is my desire to continue to write down the things I see again in my memory's eye, and the things that are today. Today I write of a cat (Eddie's book is just about finished) and not of a dog called Rover!

PANTRY

Most homes today are not built with a pantry, but in my childhood, the pantry was a key room in the house, and often Rover's bedroom!

The pantry I am about ready to describe is still in its place in the former home of my Mum and Dad. I am thinking about them today because of the phone call I received a few days ago from my sister telling me of the departure (II Timothy 4:6) of my Father (92 years young). It is funny to me that when the mind should be thinking of a person it focuses on a place associated with that person.

Our pantry wasn't that big. It was a room off the kitchen that led to the woodshed. The pantry contained extra cupboard space for all those things mother couldn't keep in the kitchen. There was an old slate sink under the only window in the pantry. It was never used to my memory, but became an extra catch-all place for ball gloves and work boots and winter mittens. In the near corner by the door to the kitchen was the wood box. It was built with an opening both in the pantry and in the woodshed. You could feed the box from the woodshed and take out the wood from the pantry. One of my jobs as a lad was to keep that wood box full; how much wood did I put in it? Across from the wood box was a counter that was used to store extra things. Under the cupboards and counters were drawers. Dad's tools and odds and ends of just about anything could be found in them. Finally, on the wall beside the door that went out into the woodshed were hangers for coats and farm cloths. I can still see Dad's coveralls and winter coats hanging on those hooks. Rover's favorite corner always contained an old discarded coat or two he used for his bedding. The pantry was also a collector of old memorabilia and many memories!

PANTRY

I can still see the huge aluminum pot sitting on the counter filled with "Blackstone Special." The pantry was a great place to chill that special homestead drink created by my mother for my sister's sixteenth birthday and thereafter made for any and all Blackstone parties. I see in my mind's eye my dog Rover sleeping in the far corner of the pantry on an old coat. In the winter months, the pantry was never heated, Rover stayed in the kitchen, but the other three seasons of the year his doghouse was the pantry. It was from the pantry window I usually saw what kind of day it would be. The windowsill usually held a few shotgun shells and a tool or two, but the view to the pasture beyond was never blocked, except when the frost was so thick you couldn't see through the window. A single light bulb hanging from the center of the ceiling was the only light in the pantry at night, but we rarely used it. The pantry was a familiar place, and was easily passed through day or dark. Besides our guard dog was always on duty in the pantry!

As I think again of that room between the kitchen and the woodshed, I am reminded of how many times I passed through it and never took notice. I was in a hurry to go nowhere, and never noticed the life that was passing me by. Now I know that I will probably never pass through that old pantry again. Once it was the portal in to the lives of Mother and Father. Father is now gone and Rover left the pantry a half century ago and how far behind is Mother? The Psalmist speaks of "**. . . thou hast set my feet in a large room.**" (Psalm 31:8) The pantry of my boyhood wasn't necessarily large but I can see now through my memories it was a large place in my youth. It was a daily exist into my world. It was also an entrance back into the safety of a loving and caring couple that for my entire life has been there for me. The pantry might have been Rover's one room in our house, but it was the gateway for all of us.

COGITATION

THE 9TH STORM OF the season has covered Ellsworth, Maine with an inch of fresh snow. It is the eighth storm that has fallen either on Saturday, Sunday, or Monday. We are in a typical Maine winter weather pattern. It is Saturday morning, and all is quiet at the parsonage across the street from where I sit once again before my computer screen to share a 'Rover' memory. As my family slept in, I finished doing the dishes for our Men's Monthly Fellowship Breakfast. The men have all left for home, or job, and the church building is once again quiet; quiet enough for meditation, or as I learned the other day, cogitation. What continues to inspire my thoughts is the time I spent on the Blackstone farm in Perham, Maine with my dog Rover.

 The boy Barry was thoughtful of the world he lived in as you have probably noticed if you have read through this series of cogitations. The love of my natural surroundings was without doubt, but cogitation was one of my strengths as a lad. Throughout my childhood, I made countless trips around the homestead, but it hasn't been till recent years I have actual pondered what I heard, saw, thought, or felt. Now these walks through the woods with Rover to the Russell Place are cherished memories down "memory lane." I only lived a mile and a half from my grandparents, two and a half miles from my school, and three miles from my church. Perham wasn't big when I was a boy, and despite its increase in population, my mind now lives in the cogitations of the 1950's and 1960's. Because I lived in a simpler day, my thoughts were simple. A small sparrow became significant; a walk to the frog pond a journey. A dog not only became my best friend, but still is the only dog I have fond memories of, and as you now know I have converted to cats. Being caught in a spring storm is remembered for

COGITATION

it symbolism, more than its shower. My thoughts of the past about the past are fond memories to this day!

 I eventually grew up and left home for a university in South Carolina. Thereafter, I migrated to New Hampshire to start my career as a small town pastor. Despite moving four times since, I have never forgotten the homeland of my birth, and the homestead of my boyhood. Time and again I find myself walking the pastureland of Perham with grandfather's Holsteins, climbing the hills that overlook Perham with Rover, strolling the banks of Salmon Brook, or looking out the barn window at a storm brewing in the eastern sky. It amazes me that what was once so insignificant now seems so full of meaning with the passage of time. Throughout these last few years, I have returned to the small agricultural town of Perham and to the unknown paradise from which my roots have sprung. Crisis has brought me back with the illness of an uncle, or mother. Decisive change has brought me back with the changing in the ownership of the land, and the selling of the homestead to the Amish. Death has brought me back with the loss of Grandfather Carroll and Grandmother Maude and Grandmother Glenna and Uncle Paul and now recently with the death of my Father Wendell. (In just a few weeks I will return again to the brow of the hill on Blackstone Road to bury my father and my 39 year old son Scott who just passed away from cancer; both Army veterans!) Back I have always come to find rejuvenation and refreshment for what lies ahead (a life without my only father and my only son), and to find inspiration from a dog called 'Rover' to press on and to go on!

 The word 'cogitation' is only used once in my old King James Version of the Bible: **"Hitherto is the end of the matter. As for me Daniel, my cogitations much trouble me, and my countenance changed in me: but I kept the matters in my heart."** (Daniel 7:28) Perhaps this is a fitting place to end this time of reminiscing about my boyhood dog Rover. According to my Hebrews lexicon 'cogitation' here means 'thoughts'; I doubt my thoughts of Rover are over, but I know as with all book projects you must stop somewhere, so like Daniel of old I guess I will keep the rest of my memories of Rover 'in my heart'!

POSTLUDE

Rover's body was clothed in black fur with the occasional spot of white. He had the strength and speed of the German-Shepherd, but the kindness and gentleness of the Border-Collie. He had a long pointed nose, and a soft appealing face, but mischief danced in his eyes. Whether roaming in the openness and vastness of pasture land, tramping and hiking through forestland, or walking in the blossoms and beauty of potato land, Rover was by my side. He loved doing anything with me, though most of the time he was more of a hindrance than a helper. Rover liked gathering eggs, or so he said, but I knew he loved chasing chickens. Rover liked feeding felines, or so he said, but I knew he loved chasing cats. Rover liked getting the Holstein herd into the barn for milking, or so he said, but I knew he loved chasing cows. Rover liked guarding the upper driveway from strangers, or so he said, but I knew he loved chasing car!

Though cats were never allowed in the large farmhouse with the side porch and connecting woodshed, Rover was, but he knew has place. The only existing picture I still have of Rover is one of him lying on a pile of coats in the corner of the kitchen by the pantry door, Rover resting place when he was inside, but Rover wasn't much of an inside dog, except in the midst of a frigid Maine winter, or towards the end of his life. Rover loved the out-of-doors like his master did, so the hardwoods of the forest were where we spent our time, not the hardwood floors of my parents' farmhouse. Rover liked everybody, and everybody liked Rover. He was an ambassador for the farm, not a guard dog. Of course, in those days you didn't need a guard dog, for family and friends were all welcome to stop in for a visit anytime, and Rover was always there to greet them. Rover was there to say goodbye when I left for school,

POSTLUDE

and he was waiting when I got off the bus from school at the top of the driveway. In the winter, he was in the kitchen when I woke in the morning, and in the summer he was in the pantry when I got ready to go do my chores. Rover was "My Best Friend", and I never replaced him when he died in a grand old, dog age; an age and a date I am ashamed to write that I have forgotten.

What you have read are to the best of my ability, fifty-five years after the fact, the facts about Rover. Is everything I have written the truth or the imagination of an old man of how it was in his boyhood? I will let my reader be the judge, but this one thing I do remember even if some of the facts are cloudy is the joy I shared with a dog named Rover in my boyhood. I have left the best for last. How did Rover get his name? In childhood, I and my friends had a game called "Red-Rover, Red Rover Send____Right Over"! Do you know the game? Two sides are chosen and then each side lines up opposite the other with hands linked with their fellow team members. One side calls out the name of a player on the other side saying: "Red-Rover, Red-Rover sends Barry right over". The player called will run to the other side trying to break through the linked arms. If they do they get to choose a player to return with them, if not they have to stay on that side until there are no members left on one side or the other. Whether or not we name Rover after the game I know not, but that is how I believe Rover: my boyhood, best friend got his name: **"A good name is rather to be chosen than great riches . . . "** (Proverbs 22:1) And I was a very rich boy indeed in my youth because I had a best friend named Rover!

Barry Blackstone-March 6, 2017

www.ingramcontent.com/pod-product-compliance
Lightning Source LLC
Chambersburg PA
CBHW070311100426
42743CB00011B/2437